A New History of Wales

THE GENTRY and the ELIZABETHAN STATE

Editors:

RALPH A. GRIFFITHS
Senior Lecturer in History
University College of Swansea

KENNETH O. MORGAN
Fellow and Praelector in Modern History
The Queen's College, Oxford

J. BEVERLEY SMITH
Senior Lecturer in Welsh History
University College of Wales, Aberystwyth

A New History of Wales

THE GENTRY and the ELIZABETHAN STATE

Gareth Jones

Christopher Davies
Swansea

© Gareth Jones

First published in 1977 by
Christopher Davies (Publishers) Ltd
4/5 Thomas Row
Swansea SA1 1NJ

ISBN 0 7154 0303 6

*Printed in Wales by
Salesbury Press Ltd
Llandybie, Dyfed*

Contents

Illustrations

For Bethan and Matthew

Acknowledgements

While some of the material in this book reflects my own research, I owe much to other historians. The bibliography draws attention to the work of some of them, but it is impossible to discharge my debt to others adequately. I can only record my gratitude in a general way. I must make special mention of the work of Dr. Penry Williams, and unpublished theses by Miss C. E. Hughes and Mr. E. G. Jones have been of great help to me. For permission to reproduce the illustrations, I am grateful to the Royal Commission on Ancient Monuments in Wales and Monmouthshire (3, 4, 6), the National Museum of Wales (1), the National Library of Wales (2), the British Library (8), the Public Record Office (7), and H. Tempest Ltd., Cardiff (5).

The three editors of this Series and Professor Glanmor Williams read the book in draft. I am deeply grateful for the care with which they did so and the valuable suggestions they made. They were responsible for drawing attention to many imperfections; but of course, they are in no way responsible for those which remain. Mrs. D. Cutler immaculately typed much of the manuscript.

Finally I wish to thank my wife for her help.

Editors' Foreword

'What is history but a nation's memory?' an eminent scholar once asked. By that test, Welsh people interested in their country's past have been suffering from an enforced loss of memory for far too long. At least until after the second world war, there was a great dearth of books on Welsh history. It seemed almost to be assumed that Wales had ceased to have a history since its conquest by Edward I, that because there was no Welsh political state there could, therefore, be no Welsh history save of the most trivial, parochial kind. Until very recently, Sir John Lloyd's great history of the Welsh people held the field almost alone — and that carried the story only down to 1282.

However, the past twenty years have witnessed a dramatic surge of interest in Welsh history in all its aspects. The importance and relevance of the history of Wales as an academic subject is now firmly established beyond dispute. A stream of important works have dealt with a wide range of historical problems, medieval and modern, ranging from the early Celtic church to the politics of the mid-twentieth century. New Welsh historical journals, some dealing with particular regions or themes, others covering Wales as a whole, have increased and multiplied, to their mutual benefit. At the national university, in other colleges, and in the schools of Wales, Welsh history has flourished as never before. It has become one of the boom subjects of our generation. And yet, all too little of this impressive upsurge of scholarship has penetrated through to the ordinary student, still less the general reader. Far too many of the fruits of Welsh historical learning have been reserved only for the benefit of other scholars, in specialist books, journals or research seminars, with only the occasional television or radio programme to whet the appetite of the layman.

A New History of Wales is designed to remedy this state of affairs fundamentally. It aims to provide a series of compact but comprehensive books which will introduce students in sixth forms, colleges and universities, and of course the general reader as well, to some of the major themes of Welsh history. It will span all aspects of the Welsh past — medieval, modern and contemporary; political, socio-economic and cultural. It will also provide, in convenient and attractive form, illustrative documents to show readers some of the kinds of source material available to the historian of Wales. Each volume will stand in its own right as a self-contained study of an important topic; there will be no attempt to impose an artificial unity on the series in general, other than its concern with Wales. The authors will be entirely free to develop their own approach; they will subscribe to no particular philosophy and will follow no special editorial blueprint. Their only brief is to be readable — and to serve the cause of historical truth as they see it. In this way, the editors hope that Welsh men and women of all ages will find new excitement in reading about their nation's past — and perhaps new incentive to ask questions about their nation's present and future.

Ralph A. Griffiths
Kenneth O. Morgan
J. Beverley Smith

Note

Numbers in the margin of the text refer to the appropriate document in the appendix. The extracts are intended to convey something of the flavour of the written materials of the period as well as to provide historical detail.

Introduction

During the night of 20 March 1559, a great storm raged in south Wales, a storm which endangered shipping in the treacherous Bristol Channel and caused considerable damage on the land bordering it. In the Vale of Glamorgan stood the castle-home of one of the most important gentlemen in the county, indeed one of the more prosperous and influential squires in the whole of Wales. Although St. Donat's Castle was built high on the land which rises steeply from the Bristol Channel, it was near enough to the sea for the noise of the storm to have been particularly frightening. The owner, Sir Thomas Stradling, can hardly have failed to be worried about the damage this storm might cause on his estate. Damage there certainly was, and the following morning John Fleming called his master to come and survey it. During their tour it was the remains of an old ash tree, blown down in the storm, that attracted Sir Thomas's attention. The trunk had cracked some seven feet above ground level, and when the top of the tree crashed to the ground it split in two, leaving the lower part still upright. It was this upright half which caught Sir Thomas's eye because there, hazel-coloured against the white of the grain, was the figure of a cross some fourteen inches high.

It would not have been difficult for Sir Thomas Stradling to have found a perfectly natural explanation for a brownish shape standing out in a tree which was probably partly rotten. But the year 1559 was some twenty years since the Reformation changes of Henry VIII's reign and the dissolution of the monasteries; only twelve years since the accession of Edward VI and the beginning of that short period when Protestantism made swift progress; only six years since Mary Tudor had begun her attempts to reverse all these religious changes; and it was only two months before Queen Elizabeth attempted a compromise which lay uneasily between Protestantism and Roman Catholicism. The religious significance of a discovery such as this would be obvious to contemporaries. But to Sir Thomas Stradling religion was of more than usual importance. The Stradling family were devoted Catholics and Sir Thomas was no exception. Since shrines and images were such an important element in Catholicism, his excitement at finding this cruciform shape is easily imagined.

The story might have ended there. Sir Thomas might well have wondered and passed on, if it had not been for the fact that he had lately received a present from his daughter, Thomasine. She was a companion of the English wife of a Spanish nobleman and was at this time in Louvain in the Spanish Netherlands. She had just sent her father 'a picture of Christ in his Resurrection'. What better present to return than a picture of this cross in the old ash tree? So Sir Thomas picked out the pattern of the cross on paper and sent the design to London to have four copies painted. Twŏ copies he gave to friends, one he sent to Thomasine and one he kept for himself. It is hardly surprising that an account of these remarkable events should spread quickly both at home and abroad. Thomasine Stradling made the details well known on the continent and it is possible that the Pope himself knew them. In Glamorgan the story spread like wildfire and many people came to see the broken-down old ash as if on pilgrimage.

No official action was taken for the present. But Sir Thomas Stradling, a justice of the peace and formerly sheriff of Glamorgan, had been in trouble with the authorities before over his staunch loyalty to Roman Catholicism. In fact, in 1551 he had been imprisoned in the Tower of London for his faith. Ten years later — two years after the discovery of the cross — the Privy Council started an investigation into the affair of the cross in the ash which resulted in his being imprisoned in the Tower once again. The Privy Council detailed two Glamorgan justices of the peace to investigate. These interviewed a number of witnesses and sent their report direct to the Council, together with the relevant pieces of the ash tree carefully wrapped in canvas. Sir Thomas was himself eventually examined by the Privy Council; he was convicted at assizes at Brentwood (Essex) in June 1561 and taken to the Tower. It is probable that only at this stage did the full consequences of his actions really dawn on him. Certainly this is the impression given in the petitions he wrote to the Queen and to the Privy Council within two days of his imprisonment. But it was not until 1563 that Sir Thomas returned to St. Donat's a free man, and then only after he had agreed to enter into a bond of 1,000 marks (a mark was 13s. 4d.) to appear before the Privy Council at twelve days' notice.

Stradling never gave up his Catholicism, even though he was an important figure in both society and government in Elizabethan Glamorgan. In 1569, at another time of national tension in political and religious affairs, he had to endure a further investigation into his behaviour. In that year there was a rising of Catholic gentlemen in northern England and, as a result, all justices of the peace in the country were made to subscribe to the act of uniformity which authorised the compromise Prayer Book of 1559. Sir Thomas refused, and this prompted an inquiry by the Privy Council. Acting in the usual way, the lords of the Council asked for a report from local justices. The report was sympathetic: Sir Thomas was old and infirm, bed-ridden with gout; he would not subscribe to the act but he was respected in the locality and, when able to do so, attended divine service regularly. The Privy Council left him to live out his last days in peace.

From the beginning of Elizabeth's reign, we move to the end. In the autumn of 1601 an election was held to elect the M.P. for Denbighshire. Not for the first time was there trouble. In 1558 there had been trickery and double-dealing at the election of the knight of the shire for Denbighshire and a long, complicated court case followed in the court of Star Chamber. Now, in 1601, the old rivalry between the families of the eastern and western parts of the county was sparked off again. The leading personalities in the struggle were, in the east, Sir Richard Trevor of Trefalun and Sir John Lloyd of Bodidras; in the west, Sir John Salusbury of Lleweni. These men were already at loggerheads as to who should have precedence as J.P. in the county. Then came the election which gave an opportunity for the quarrel to be even more bitterly contested. It seemed that

Salusbury was in an unbeatable position, since by far the largest number of electors lived in west Denbighshire, but Trevor and Lloyd had the sheriff on their side and he was the returning officer at elections. Indeed, Salusbury accused the sheriff of hiding the election writ until the county court, where the election was to take place, could be held in Wrexham, a town which was not under Salusbury's influence.

Nevertheless, the situation seemed desperate for the easterners when, four days before the election, their candidate decided to drop out. Sir Richard Trevor was himself now forced to stand. At this crucial moment orders arrived from the Privy Council requiring that sixty men be mustered for military service in Ireland. Two days before the election Trevor held his muster in Wrexham. The only men he nominated for Irish service were those who had refused to support him in the election or whose masters had refused their support. The procedure by which he did this was quite illegal but effective:forty men who would have voted for Trevor's opponent were prevented from doing so.

The election itself proved to be remarkable even by Elizabethan standards. Preparations on both sides involved large quantities of weapons, Trevor bringing in pikes from Chester, and Salusbury's men (so Trevor alleged) being armed with daggers, swords, pistols and staves. According to some of the evidence, there were hundreds of armed men in Wrexham the evening before the election. Both that evening and the day of the election, 21 October 1601, the sheriff attempted to get the two sides to compromise but Salusbury, it seems, was determined to fight to the bitter end. The sheriff decided that to hold the county court in the shire hall was impossible because of the large numbers of armed followers on both sides and the consequent likelihood of violence. He decided, therefore, to hold the court out in the open. As it turned out, the presence of a multitude of armed men — perhaps as many as three hundred in the churchyard alone — did not lead to rioting. The only violence came when Trevor and Salusbury met at the churchyard. They drew their swords, a shot was fired, but courageous action by the sheriff and his men in separating the two sides prevented a large-scale fight.

The day had seen a considerable amount of action but the main purpose of the proceedings, the election of an M.P., was not achieved. The sheriff said that the danger of death and injury was too great. It was only on 16 December 1601 that Sir John Salusbury was eventually elected, by which time the parliamentary session had almost ended. The Privy Council, always sensitive to major feuds like this, tried to restore some kind of peaceful relationship between the contestants by interviewing them in London, but both sides eventually took their cases to the court of Star Chamber.

These two episodes in the history of Elizabethan Wales shed light on several aspects of the gentry's involvement in government. Institutions of government such as the Privy Council and Star Chamber provided (as we shall see in Chapter III) the framework within which the gentry worked as local officials. The apparatus of government depended upon the involvement and co-operation of the gentry at local and often at regional level. Without this, Elizabethan government would have collapsed. Furthermore, the Privy Council and Star Chamber provided the opportunity for a marginally more peaceful and lawful existence for those families who,while pursuing their rivalries as keenly as ever, did so in the knowledge that there were institutions of government able to discipline the most influential of the queen's subjects. At the same time, it must be remembered that these were the ultimate constraints which the state could impose. Usually the Privy Council intervened in personal feuds only when other machinery had failed and Star Chamber was often the last resort for those who had not obtained justice in lesser courts. Cases which eventually reached Star Chamber and the other Westminster courts had often involved the use of force or ingenious chicanery.

Secondly, the two episodes introduce some of the officials of county government, such as sheriffs and J.P.s. It was county government which (as we shall see in Chapter IV) gave the more important gentry their opportunity to participate in relatively large numbers in administration and justice in the period after the act of Union. The majority of gentry families seized these opportunities eagerly, though with mixed motives. They were influenced·by the power and prestige that office-holding conferred on them. For some there was an acceptance of the Renaissance philosophy that it was the duty of a gentleman to participate in the government of his country. For others office-holding provided opportunity to abuse the privileges which went with office by means of corruption and the blatantly illegal pursuit of family rivalries. For most there was something of all these motives involved.

Thirdly, the events in Glamorgan and Denbighshire point to two spheres of recurring conflict in the Elizabethan period, religion and politics, with politics not a matter of party but of personal relationships, influence and prestige. These conflicts, and others which we shall consider, point to the stresses associated with the position of the gentry as both governors and governed. The first task, however, must be to see this role in its historical and social perspective.

Chapter I

The Problem of Government

The historian of Tudor Wales is fortunate in that a number of
gentlemen wrote about the society in which they lived and their
writings furnish invaluable historical information. But, as with
so many historical sources, the insights they provide unwittingly into their own attitudes are often of even greater
value. The sixteenth century was something of a watershed in
the writing of history. On the one hand, Polydore Vergil to
some extent anticipated the development of a more scientific
approach to history by questioning many of the historical
myths which were popular in the sixteenth century. On the
other hand, there was the remarkably widespread interest in the
history and topography of Britain which prompted the travels
of, for example, Leland and Camden. Elizabethan Wales produced its fair share of antiquaries. David Powel, rector of
Ruabon, published *The Historie of Cambria* in 1584. Sir
Edward Stradling of St. Donat's wrote a version of the Norman
Conquest of Glamorgan which has misled historians down to
the present century. Sir John Wynn of Gwydir wrote the history of his family; and Rice Merrick, clerk of the peace in Glamorgan, produced his *Booke of Glamorganshires Antiquities*.
Merrick represented those gentry who valued the study of the
past and the recording of the present. These interests were
prompted partly by the social rewards that came from a res-
pectable pedigree, partly by the need to establish a title to the
lands of a gentleman, and partly by a real love of scholarship.
Rice Merrick read the various works of Leland, Camden and

other Tudor antiquaries, consulted the works of fellow Welsh-men, Sir John Price and Humphrey Lluyd, sought diligently for historical documents, and took oral evidence from some of the older inhabitants of Glamorgan. His important book of pedigrees has unfortunately not survived, but his remarkable account of the history of Glamorgan and its Norman families, with a topographical survey of part of the county, is an invaluable source for the historian.

One of the outstanding historians of Elizabethan Wales was George Owen. As one of the most prosperous of Pembrokeshire gentlemen, lord of Cemaes and a public servant, he will figure prominently in later pages. He was also a genealogist and antiquary of outstanding industry and skill. He was interested in the history, geography and geology of Pembrokeshire in particular, but also of the rest of Wales. What he wrote on these subjects is of great importance; his description of life in Pembrokeshire — its agriculture and coalmining, its lack of enclosures, its lack of schools and the poverty of its preachers, its recreations — is invaluable. But anyone studying the government of Elizabethan Wales must give primacy to Owen's *Dialogue of the Government of Wales,* where he described in detail the institutions of government from the Council in the Marches to the hundred and manorial courts. One example will illustrate just how important the *Dialogue* is. The Council in the Marches was both an administrative body and a court. Its administrative records survive; its judicial records generally do not. Therefore, George Owen's comments on this side of the Council's work assume great importance.

Writers like George Owen and Sir John Wynn serve the historian in another way. By their selection of subject and material, by their commentary on the history of Wales, they unwittingly reveal much about themselves and their class. Both Owen and Wynn paint a black picture of pre-Tudor government, emphasising the lawlessness of fifteenth-century Welsh society. George Owen is more specific than Wynn. He writes of a Wales in 'trouble' and 'chaos' before the coming of the Tudors in 1485. He wrote at length about King Henry IV's penal legislation (1401-2) against the Welsh, designed not only for their punishment, but also to deprive them of all liberty and freedom, and to bar them from all civil Education. That they should not dwell or be brought up in any City or Town, that they should not be [able to inherit] in any Town, or bear any office of credit or trust were it never so mean, and diverse other Laws loathsome to recite.. . .

Then came the moment when Henry Tudor delivered Wales from its sorry state. George Owen compares the Welsh with 'the children of Israel under the whip of the merciless taskmasters of Egypt' before God 'sent unto us a Moses that delivered us from bondage'. No praise is too high for the deliverer. Owen says that at a time when English and Welsh despised each other,

> it pleased the lord of his mercy to send us a Prince of our own Nation and born in our Country to govern both England and Wales; I mean that worthy and grave Prince Henry the seventh, who for his wisdom is termed in histories of foreign nations a second Solomon.

This, to George Owen, was the 'joyful Metamorphosis' wrought by the Tudors. Out of the turbulence, chaos and servility of fifteenth-century Wales emerged the good government and just society of the sixteenth century, consolidated by Henry VII's 'good and pleasant' laws for the 'good government of the country'.

Historians do not now see the Tudors as miracle workers. They emphasise the continuity between late-medieval and early-modern history. They stress the use which Henry VII made of established institutions of government, play down the Tudor 'revolution' in government, draw attention to the continuing power of the nobility and the Crown's dependence on them; and they see the political stability of the Elizabethan state as very largely dependent on the queen's longevity. George Owen, Sir John Wynn and Rice Merrick were landed gentry. They saw sixteenth-century history from the point of view of a class which owed much of its prosperity and prestige to the Tudors. It is hardly surprising that they viewed the act of Union so favourably. Landed estates had been gradually, often painfully, created through an increasing acceptance of English land law in medieval Wales. The act of Union eased the process along by abolishing partible succession. Such estate building had already been helped considerably by the fact that Welshmen had been accepting offices under the Crown, thereby fulfilling a vital role in the government of fourteenth- and fifteenth-century Wales. In fact, the Crown had long depended on those families who successfully evaded the legislation of Henry IV. Those gentry who benefited most from the act of Union naturally regarded the Tudors as benefactors and emphasised the contrast between the part-Welsh Henry Tudor and the seemingly oppressive Henry IV. Inevitably, they would point the contrast between the lawlessness of medieval Wales and the law-abiding nature of Tudor society. These were the very people entrusted with ensuring good government and, not surprisingly, they felt they were doing a good job. Therefore, we have to look critically at the picture they painted of Tudor Wales and try to reconcile it with the considerable evidence that this was not a society in which the problems of law enforcement were largely solved.

Any assessment of the success or failure of Elizabethan government in Wales must be seen in a wider context than that indicated by contemporary historians. It must, for example, be seen in the context of the government and society of England and Wales as a whole. Politics and society were still dominated by the aristocracy. They normally supported the Crown and the Crown relied on this support in a crisis. Magnates still kept large numbers of retainers and enjoyed considerable military power. Even when the office of lord lieutenant and the militia system of recruitment (a form of conscription) emerged from the crises of the 1540s and 1550s, this aristocratic military power was not swept away. It was the aristocracy, acting as lords lieutenant, who carried out the duty of recruitment.

The aristocracy exercised the greatest political power in Elizabethan England and Wales. They maintained power and influence by those complicated political manoeuvrings and intrigues which are so characteristic of the Elizabethan Court. They owed their pre-eminence to a combination of noble birth, wealth and office. but it was essential for them to preserve a power base in the country as well as at Court. It was this that lay at the root of the faction struggles of the Elizabethan period and ensured that the magnates were often at the centre of disruption in the localities. Power was at stake and both magnates and gentry were ruthless in pursuing it.

The history of faction in Wales is particularly complicated. Following Penry Williams, we can divide Elizabeth's reign into the period up to 1588, when there were some six dominant families in Wales, and the period after 1588, when this number fell to three. Up to 1588 men with influence at Court and large estates in the country had massive influence in the Welsh counties: Sir John Perrot in Pembrokeshire, the earl of Worcester in Monmouthshire, the earl of Essex in Carmarthenshire, the earls of Pembroke in Glamorgan, the earl of Leicester in north Wales. The last of these was the most powerful of all. Robert Dudley, earl of Leicester and a favourite of Queen Elizabeth, was one of the most powerful men in the country and his influence at Court could always be put to good advantage. As lord of Denbigh and owner of extensive estates in Denbighshire, and as commissioner to investigate lands in north Wales which had been illegally taken over by local gentry, he had immense economic power over the gentry and freeholders.

The other common method of building up influence was through the friendship and support of other important families, and Leicester had a solid group of clients. This had been fostered largely through the influence of his close relative, Sir Henry Sidney who, as lord president of the Council in the Marches, had vast resources of patronage, and of the Wynns of Gwydir, the most influential gentry family in Caernarvonshire. It is an important (and relevant) feature of faction that the power and authority of even influential men such as these did not go unchallenged. There was always opposition, usually from other old-established, wealthy or prominent families with the resources to put up a fight. In this case, it was Sir Richard Bulkeley of Beaumaris who fought to preserve his own influence in the locality in the face of particularly powerful competition. He did not lack support in resisting Leicester's encroachments.

Related to Leicester by marriage was Henry Herbert, earl of Pembroke, the most important of the south Wales magnates. The Pembroke family had large estates in Wiltshire and, through Henry's father, Sir William Herbert (made earl of Pembroke in 1551), were lords of Glamorgan and owners of the largest estate in that county. Henry Herbert, the second earl, thus had a particularly sound economic base for his power in Wales. We can add to it his influence at Court as one of Leicester's supporters and relatives, and the position he occupied after 1586 as lord president of the Council in the Marches. He had no qualms about using this power in Glamorgan in local politics and military arrangements — indeed, wherever he felt his position as lord of Glamorgan to be in any way threatened; and he tended to regard the borough of Cardiff as his personal property. It was his attempts to exercise the rights of a marcher lord which largely dictated the pattern of politics in the county, but he did not have it all his own way, influential though he was. There were other powerful families in Glamorgan who were not afraid to oppose him, notably the Mansels and the Stradlings.

Faction was made even more complex by the network of family relationships among the aristocracy and gentry. Here again Pembroke's family provides us with a good example. In Glamorgan there were numerous branches of the Herberts — in Swansea, Neath, Cogan Pill and Cardiff. Those in Swansea and Cardiff were particularly influential. But the earl's relatives were found far outside the county boundaries, particularly in Monmouthshire and Montgomeryshire. There was a much greater degree of inter-relationship among the gentry even than this, because they intermarried with great frequency. This was not only socially inevitable but was encouraged by economic and political considerations. Good marriages were an important way of building up a sound economic base and influence in a locality. A good example of how complex such networks could be is provided by the Gamages of Coity, near Bridgend. The family was related to the important Stradling family of St. Donat's, to the Crofts of Herefordshire, who had considerable influence at Elizabeth's Court, and to such pro-

25

minent personalities as Lord Howard of Effingham and Sir Walter Raleigh.

At first sight, the family trees of the gentry might not appear to have much bearing on the study of Elizabethan government, but in fact family relationships were fundamental to many aspects of contemporary life. For example, they ensured that Elizabeth's Court sometimes became involved in local matters through the influence of men such as Pembroke, Leicester and Essex. They ensured, too, that all local appointments had significance in the 'power-game' that was played constantly by the various factions. When the earl of Pembroke was president of the Council in the Marches, Herberts were appointed to deputy-lieutenancies (the most prestigious of county offices) in Glamorgan, Monmouthshire and Montgomeryshire. In north Wales, the influence of the earls of Leicester and Essex was crucial both to the appointment of local officials and in the attitude of the gentry to each faction. Furthermore, it meant that the kind of rivalries which existed between families and 'influences' was harmful to good government. Many of the episodes of violence and riot which so often mark relations between the gentry can be put down to family rivalries. In the 1570s and 1580s, for example, the earl of Pembroke's influence in Glamorgan was fairly consistently opposed by the Mansels. This antagonism was paralleled in other Welsh counties. Sometimes disputes arose between the gentry of the east and those of the west of a county like Denbighshire. In north Wales as a whole the major influence in determining family loyalties was that of the earls of Leicester and Essex. In all counties feuds could — and often did — break out into violence between the retainers of the major families.

The machinations of the aristocracy and complex family ties among the gentry introduced two complicating factors into local government. A third was the relationship between gentry and community. For example, retainers did not suddenly disappear from Tudor Wales and the more substantial families could command the service of scores of men. They were as much a hazard to good order as they had ever been. Gentlemen also exercised a considerable hold over the loyalty of their tenants and, indeed, of the wider community. Under Elizabeth I the gentry were the natural leaders in the community. Their role gave cohesion to a wider society. As landlords the gentry sometimes protected the interests of their tenants, and this could bring them into conflict with other families. But conflict could also arise with tenants, as, for example, when rents were raised in the inflationary conditions of the sixteenth century.

It was against this complex back-cloth, as well as within the framework laid down by the act of Union, that the county gentlemen assumed responsibility for the good government of Elizabethan Wales. We must take account of the many conflicting pressures upon them when we try to judge the success or failure of this government.

Chapter II

Governing Families

Gentry involvement in local government was not, as is sometimes supposed, brought about by the act of Union. Some of the offices which they held after the act was passed were familiar in name and, to some extent, in function centuries before. For example, the office of sheriff was an ancient one dating back to Anglo-Saxon times, and in medieval Wales it was particularly important since in some counties it carried with it powers of administration, finance and justice. When the statute of Rhuddlan settled the government of the principality of north Wales in 1284, the shrievalty became an important and integral part of the new régime. In west Wales the sheriff was much less important, but he was, nevertheless, involved in the kind of police functions of executing writs, empanelling juries and dealing with prisoners which were his staple duties in the Elizabethan period.

Not only were some of the offices of Elizabethan administration not new, but office-holding by gentlemen was no novelty. In north Wales there can be no doubting the increasing participation of Welshmen in local government in the middle ages nor the consequent alliance of many important families with the Crown. Even the dislocation resulting from the revolt of Owain Glyndŵr at the beginning of the fifteenth century was to prove only temporary. During the course of the fifteenth century, when the difficulties of English kings became greater, Welshmen penetrated to an ever increasing extent the ranks of office holders. Nominally the great offices of Welsh government were usually in the hands of Englishmen; in practice, these men were often absent from Wales for long periods and Welshmen became the real rulers of the country.

In south Wales, too, there were great opportunities for gentry families in the fifteenth century. The withdrawal of several marcher lords, combined with long periods of weak kingship, produced openings for Welsh families. For example, Gruffydd ap Nicholas, Sir Rhys ap Thomas's grandfather, became deputy justiciar of Carmarthenshire and Cardiganshire. It is true that the justiciar's power was in decline in the fifteenth century, but this was still an office of considerable importance. In fact, holding office, at all but the highest levels, was one important method by which families could improve their prospects and make a name for themselves. The changes which were brought about by the act of Union were considerable and they provided opportunities on a much wider scale for the gentry, but the determination of gentlemen to seize these opportunities and make themselves responsible for local government was nothing new. It was just that, by Elizabeth's reign, the sources of power in the counties of Wales were more clearly defined. There was now no disputing the dependence of the central government, of Crown and Privy Council, on the county gentry for the good government of Wales.

Nevertheless, ultimate authority rested with the queen and the institutions of central government. This meant that the gentry, important as their rôle was, had their freedom of action circumscribed by the aristocracy who dominated these institutions. The gentry could work only within the framework of the ever-present national and local influence of the aristocracy. This is particularly true in the Elizabethan period; however much it may be argued that there had been a shift in power to the gentry. As we have seen, the Welsh counties, no less than the English, were affected by the complicated jockeying for position among the nobility. Fortunes could be made as a result of favours from the queen, but political power was the real prize. The power of an earl of Leicester or an earl of Essex was based to a considerable extent on a network of allegiances which extended into many parts of England and Wales. These allegiances were fostered by patronage and influence involving aristocratic and gentry families. The meteoric rise of William Herbert, earl of Pembroke in mid-century altered the whole balance of political power in Wales; the influence of the aristocracy, old and new, has always to be borne in mind.

There is little problem in recognising the Elizabethan aristocracy; their titles are sufficient indication of status. Not so with the gentry. Historians' definitions are legion; but none is completely satisfactory. The Welsh gentry encompass a range of background, wealth and interest which probably defies definition. A gentleman had to have an income from land; but in Wales it might be remarkably modest by English standards and possibly less than that of a prosperous yeoman. If he was a knight or bore arms there was no doubt of his gentry status; but the majority of the Welsh gentry had to rely on as impressive a pedigree as they could lay claim to — or fabricate. This lack of homogeneity is not surprising. The Welsh gentry were of remarkably diverse origins. Some were descended from the princes of Wales or those who served them; others from the official class which grew up in the principalities of north and south Wales. 'During the fourteenth century', wrote Glyn Roberts, 'they appear as bailiffs of commotes, escheators, deputy sheriffs, and recipients of leases of Crown rights . . .' There were families of native Welsh gentry who could trace their early rise to the participation of their ancestors in marcher government as seneschals, for example. Yet others of the Welsh gentry were of Norman or English stock; they were usually found in the more fertile parts of Wales, as, for example, the Stradlings, Bassets and Turbervilles of the vale of Glamorgan or the Salusbury family of Denbighshire. By Elizabeth's reign they had long been integrated with those of Welsh origin.

The beginnings of many of these families can be traced to fourteenth-century Wales, but it was really the fifteenth century which saw the transformation of Welsh society. Ogwen Williams's generalisations concerning Caernarvonshire serve to make the point for many areas.

> Roughly between 1460 and 1550 . . . a revolution in landowner-
> ship may, perhaps, be said to have taken place as land, loosened

from the hold of its medieval organisation, became available for exploitation and possession by a new kind of landed proprietor. Its main social consequences were twofold. Undei the medieval system a man, whether free or bond, had normally enjoyed during his lifetime an allotted stake in the land. Now, at the beginning of the sixteenth century . . . society in Caernarvonshire became basically divided into two classes, one consisting of families who owned land and property and the other of landless men. Secondly, whereas in Welsh medieval society the basic motive governing economic activity had been the production of food and the necessities of life for the benefit of a communal unit . . . in Tudor society the basic motive was the making of individual incomes in cash.

There were diverse reasons for the growth of this gentry class. In Glyn Roberts's words, 'in Marches and Principality alike, the holding of office was a major factor in the growth of the gentry class'. It was the gentry, not the aristocracy as in England, who did much of the routine work of government in fourteenth- and fifteenth-century Wales, Henry IV's penal legislation notwithstanding. With office went rewards, particularly the opportunity to lease or purchase land, sometimes as a result of royal favour. Another pre-condition of the growth of individual estates was the disintegration of tribal society, a process quickened by the Black Death and the Glyndŵr revolt. The Church provided an avenue of advance, as also did war and trade. With the accession of Henry VII royal favour was the reward of those who had backed the winner at the battle of Bosworth (Rhys ap Thomas being the outstanding example), and Welshmen generally came into royal favour. During the sixteenth century the gentry were presented with new opportunities to consolidate their position. The dissolution of the monasteries was the greatest: the élite among the gentry leased or bought monastic land on a big scale but lesser gentlemen were also in the market. Monastic land and Crown land constantly changed hands throughout the sixteenth century, a reminder that the process of estate-building was a major pre-occupation of the gentry. The ranks of that class were not immutable: some prospered, some went to the wall. Inflation, which saw prices rise as much as five-fold over the century, provided opportunities and pitfalls. The nature of the terrain played a vital part in the balance of wealth in Wales: the vale of Glamorgan or parts of Pembrokeshire provided opportunities for intensive and prosperous farming, both of land and livestock, which were not available in the hilly counties. Consolidation of estates was impossible without good luck. If there was no male heir, the family name was doomed and the estate swallowed up by other, more fortunate, landowners.

The gentry of Elizabethan Wales were remarkable for their diversity of wealth, property and life-style. They farmed a few acres or tens of manors. They lived in castles, carefully converted to suit the demands of the Elizabethan period, or in long cottages. Ogwen Williams estimated that the minimum income from land of a Caernarvonshire gentleman in the 1540s was £3 per annum. Sir John Perrot of Carew, one of the wealthiest of the gentry in Elizabeth's reign, had an income from land of £850 per annum — though figures of this kind have to take into account the high inflation rate of the sixteenth century.

Generalisations about the role of the Welsh gentry in government cannot encompass the whole spectrum of wealth and status. Historians writing about the gentry have used various sub-groupings which might be relevant to the subject of office-holding. J. T. Cliffe, in his study of the Yorkshire gentry, used a three-fold division, with the upper gentry holding leading offices in the county such as M.P., deputy lieutenant and sheriff; while the middle rank could aspire to the commission of the peace. Penry Williams has suggested that such a division could profitably be used in looking at Tudor Glamorgan. In Elizabeth's reign there were some six families who occupied a pre-eminent position in the affairs of this county and filled the highest òffices. Below them came some forty families whose heads might become J.P.s. The third layer was formed by dozens of minor gentry, difficult to distinguish from prosperous yeomen. In his analysis of the social structure of Tudor Caernarvonshire, Ogwen Williams made the distinction between a gentleman and an esquire.

> An esquire was really a landed gentleman on a grander scale. His pedigree was often no better than that of a gentleman or yeo-

man; his speech and manners were probably as rough and ready
as theirs. But he was living in or was building . . . a larger and
more pretentious house . . . He was a considerable landowner . . .
He was a rich man in the community in which he lived . . .
Common estimation of his status based upon wealth and land-
ownership was reinforced by the fact that he was often a justice
of the peace or had served as sheriff of the county. Sometimes
the honour of knighthood was conferred on him, a valuable but-
tress of his social position.

Since our concern in this study lies with the important offices
in local government and their holders, the problem of definition hardly arises. Almost invariably we encounter at all points
the upper stratum of gentlemen from whose ranks were drawn
the deputy-lieutenants, sheriffs and J.P.s. They held the courts
and served on special commissions. It was their misdemeanours which caused a major stir because the government knew
full well how vital was their role. We can now examine in more
detail how some heads of gentry families had achieved a position of pre-eminence in Elizabethan Wales.

We have already encountered George Owen of Henllys in
Pembrokeshire, antiquary, genealogist and historian; but his
literary activities filled only a part of his life. Like all Elizabethan gentlemen, his first concern was consolidation and en-
largement of his estates; and he also had to meet a variety of responsibilities in local government. Following B. G. Charles, we
can examine Owen's background in some detail. It seems only
just that a man of Owen's skill as a genealogist should have a
genuine pedigree dating back to the twelfth century, though his
claim to be descended from the princely house of Deheubarth
was spurious. The Owen estate was built up slowly and pains-
takingly, with the occasional spurt as a result of advantageous
marriages. The early Tudor period saw Rhys ab Owain Fychan
consolidating the Henllys estate, and by 1497 he was already
designated a 'gentleman'. His son, William Owen, had a legal
training at the Middle Temple in London and settled in Pembroke, where he held a number of offices. At various times he
was mayor of Pembroke, joint steward and receiver of the shire
of Pembroke and controller of the ports of Pembroke, Haverfordwest and Tenby. The most significant of Owen's achieve-

ments, however, was to become lord of Cemais. The previous lord had got himself deeply in debt, mortgaging his Cemais lands to Owen. Eventually, Owen acquired these lands outright and, given the good sense and judgement which was notably lacking in his predecessor, his own and his family's fortunes were assured; but William Owen did not rest there. The process of estate building in Tudor Wales was sometimes spectacular, as when large portions of monastic or Crown land were acquired by major families; but normally it was a gradual, continuous process of land accumulation on a small scale. To this end Owen bought out as many of his freehold neighbours as he could. He married well. His second wife was Elizabeth, niece of the earl of Pembroke and daughter of Sir George Herbert of Swansea. William Owen's social standing was yet more secure as a result; and another important link between gentry families was forged.

George Owen was in many ways typical of that top layer of Welsh gentry who were so vital to the government and administration of their county and country. He inherited status and a large estate; but he made the best of his advantages. In B. G. Charles's words, 'He was industrious, thrifty, ambitious and far-sighted . . . The process of building up a freehold estate around Henllys, begun by his father, was vigorously pursued...' From his writings we know of his progressive methods of farming. He preached and practised enclosure. He used fertilisers — limestone, marl and seaweed; he discussed their merits at length in his writings.

He too married well. His first wife was that most coveted of women, an heiress — the daughter of William Phillips of Picton. George's fortune and social standing were greatly enhanced by this alliance with one of the leading Pembrokeshire families. It also helped to cement Owen's allegiance in the politics of Elizabethan Pembrokeshire. Both Phillips and Owen were leaders of a group of families who opposed that most influential of the county gentry, Sir John Perrot. The implications of this power struggle in Pembrokeshire were far-reaching because of the clashes which resulted. One of the most interesting has been recounted in detail by B. G. Charles. A market day in Haverfordwest provided the occasion for a possible riot between armed retainers of the two factions. As it turned out there was no clash, but the sheriff, who was pro-Perrot, ordered the arrest of two of George Owen's men. Rees Jenkin Awbrey of Newport, 'by repute . . . a card-player, a frequenter of taverns and an associate of a thieving woman', was clapped in gaol. Rees Gwyneth of Nevern, 'a one-eyed North Walian with something of a reputation for horse-stealing, even of murder', managed to escape to the house of an Owen supporter.

> The sheriff's men pursued him up the stairs and at the top of the second flight were confronted by William Philipps himself, his strongest adherent John Barlow of Slebech who had a long-lasting feud against Perrot . . . and George Owen. Alban Stepney arrived shortly afterwards. When told that they had no right to arrest the man within the town liberties, the sheriff's officers had to retire with their tails between their legs. But a crowd had gathered outside; only a spark of temper was needed to start a row. To avoid trouble the mayor was summoned to the scene and, being a partisan of the anti-Perrot faction, he was only too ready to put the under-sheriff in the town gaol for infringing the rights of the borough. If either of the parties scored over the other that day, it was not Perrot's. Owen and his men trudged home through the snows of Prescely without great loss of prestige.

It is surprising to recall at the end of this story that George Owen played a prominent part in government and peace-keeping in his county; it is certainly paradoxical that he applied himself seriously as a J.P. from about 1584, as sheriff of the county twice, deputy-lieutenant for several years and deputy vice-admiral. As J.P. he applied his probing mind to the problem of sheep-stealing; and he got the Council in the Marches to accept his suggestions for regulating and registering sheep ear-markings. He was deputy-lieutenant in a county with which the central government was particularly concerned because of the threat of invasion through Milford Haven. Although the deputy-lieutenants were not always at hand to perform their duties properly, there is no doubt that Owen and his fellows put a lot of effort into organising the military defences of Pembrokeshire. They were also responsible for raising money for armour and caring for it. Often it was kept in gentry houses, but one of Owen's proud achievements was to build an armoury house to serve that part of the county for which he was particularly responsible. He also played his part in interrogating Spanish sailors whose ships were wrecked off the west coast of Wales and in caring for wounded sailors returning from the Irish wars.

When we add George Owen's literary achievements to those of estate manager and public servant, we realise how wide-ranging were his activities and talents. He was a man of considerable intellect and ability. But he was also a child of his age and therefore not untypical of that class which was presented with economic, administrative and educational opportunities of immense potential in Elizabethan Wales.

The Vaughans of Golden Grove in Carmarthenshire had the advantage over the Owens of Henllys in that they could claim descent from the twelfth-century prince of Powys, Madog ap Maredudd, through one of his illegitimate sons. In the late-fifteenth century Hugh Vaughan became the first of the family to settle in south Wales. In Francis Jones's words,

> The few glimpses that have survived relating to Hugh Vaughan indicate that he had taken those preliminary steps by which so many Welsh families established their position at this time. Loyalty to the Crown, the acceptance of relatively minor official posts which gave local prestige and provided a starting point to higher things, finally sealed with a court appointment — here was the well-known pattern governing the re-emergence of the long-pedigreed native élite from centuries of turbulence and uncertainty, burgeoning in Tudor times into energetic, enterprising gentry in whose hands local government and parliamentary representation remained until the latter half of the nineteenth century.

Hugh Vaughan followed the familiar pattern in other ways. There was a highly advantageous marriage to a relative of Sir Rhys ap Thomas. There was the growth and consolidation of a large estate by Hugh and his son John, the process being accelerated by the acquisition of leases of Rhys ap Gruffydd's lands. But the process of estate-building was concentrated particularly in the period 1540-70.

John Vaughan followed the family precedent of public service — as M.P., sheriff and J.P. His son, Walter Vaughan, was head of what was probably the foremost family in Carmarthenshire. He, too, married well; by one marriage Sir John Perrot of Carew became his father-in-law. John held the same office as his father and was one of the founders of Carmarthen Grammar School. Nor did he neglect the family fortunes. He added to the estate and exploited coalmines in Llangennech, Llwynhendy and Kidwelly. He gave his eldest son an education which was typical of his class and period, for young John Vaughan went to Jesus College, Oxford, favoured by so many Welsh families, and entered the Inns of Court. He played a prominent part in Carmarthenshire's affairs and eventually became earl of Carbery in Charles I's reign.

The Stradling family of St. Donat's in Glamorgan furnish another example of the variety of background and range of interest of the more prominent gentry families. They were one of the half-dozen or so wealthiest and most powerful Glamorgan gentry; they were long established, too, having come from Somerset in Edward I's reign. Writing in the sixteenth century and reflecting the contemporary obsession with ancestry, Sir Edward Stradling traced his family's roots back to the Norman Conquest and to the mythical Sir William le Esterling. But the first Stradling to settle in Glamorgan was in fact Sir Peter Stradling, who, at the end of the thirteenth century, married Joan de Hawey, heiress to estates which included St. Donat's. This union was the start of an association with Glamorgan which was to last until the early-eighteenth century. During the middle ages the head of the family was frequently a person deeply devoted to religion. Sir William Stradling went on pilgrimage to Rome in 1408 and his son Edward died on a pilgrimage to Jerusalem. A similar fate befell his son, Sir Harry Stradling, who died in Cyprus on the return journey from the Holy Land. Such elements in the family's history help to explain Sir Thomas Stradling's strong Roman Catholic sympathies. And yet the family fortunes do not seem to have been adversely affected by these sympathies during the Reformation, and religion played an altogether less controversial part in the life of the next head of the family, Sir Edward Strad-ling. He lived at St. Donat's for almost the whole of Elizabeth's reign and was probably the most accomplished of all the Strad-lings. He was not, of course, the founder of the family fortunes. The estates had been built up over centuries and wise marriages, which were so important in the economy and politics of the period, had played a crucial part from the early days. The Stradlings had also profited from the land 'bonanza' created by the dissolution of the monasteries. They bought up some lands in Glamorgan which had formerly belonged to Tewkesbury Abbey. So Sir Edward Stradling inherited a profitable Glam-organ estate of eleven manors. He continued to make it pay in one of the most inflationary periods in British history and doubtless deserved his reputation as a highly competent estate manager. His reputation, however, does not lie in any one par-ticular achievement but rather in the variety of his interests. In-heritor of a castle which occupies one of the most beautiful sites in the county, he added a wing in the typical Elizabethan style and made other improvements which transformed the late-medieval castle into a less austere Elizabethan mansion. He was a notable scholar who seems to have profited more than most from his Oxford education and travels abroad. He carried on the family tradition of patronage of Welsh poets, bore the expense of publishing Dr. Sion Dafydd Rhys's book of Welsh grammar, and was a keen collector of ancient manuscripts and books which he built up into a superb library. He knew William Cecil well and was related to such notables as Lord Howard of Effingham and Francis Walsingham. From his famous deer park came some of the best venison in Wales and his table made him renowned for his generous hospitality. It followed inevitably that a man of his means, ability and position in the county should play an important role in the government of Elizabethan Glamorgan.

The Wynns of Gwydir, in Caernarvonshire, were the best known of a number of branches of the Wynn family in north Wales, and Sir John Wynn (1553-1627) is only the most out-standing of a family which made a considerable impact on local affairs in the Tudor period. Sir John's grandfather, John ap

Maredudd, had rebuilt Gwydir, the family mansion, in 1555. He served as both M.P. and sheriff of Caernarvonshire, a sure indication of his important position in the county. His son, Maurice, followed in his footsteps, four times as M.P., three times as sheriff.

Maurice's son was Sir John Wynn, among the best known of a famous family. This is partly due to the fact that his *History of the Gwydir Family* is one of the most important contemporary sources of information relating to the Tudor gentry. It is due also to his importance in his native county, where his position as the leader of political and official life was hardly challenged. He was, in fact, typical of the higher ranks of the gentry else where. He received the best education available at the time, at All Souls College, Oxford, and at the Inns of Court in London. He had sufficient money to live in London for long periods. When his father died in 1580 he inherited a large and profitable estate and he was determined to enlarge it and make it more profitable whenever the opportunity arose. The frequent court cases in which he was involved show how jealously he guarded his title to land. In other ways, too, he was typical of the Elizabethan gentry. He was closely involved in all aspects of the political and official life of Caernarvonshire and neighbouring counties. He was sheriff on five occasions, twice of Caernarvonshire, twice of Merionethshire and once of Denbighshire. He was elected once as M.P. for Caernarvonshire and, in 1608, was appointed to the Council in the Marches. Many of the Elizabethan gentry added to their wealth by responding to the increased demand for fuel — especially timber and coal — and by developing the small industries (for example, iron) of the period. Sir John Wynn was no exception. He had interests in the important Parys Mountain copper mines in Anglesey and tried to introduce the manufacture of Welsh friezes into the vale of Conway. He had other, more philanthropic interests and activities, too. He was, like Sir Edward Stradling, an author of ability and he encouraged local poets. His family later liked to think that he had founded a school in Llanrwst, though there is some doubt as to whether he actually provided the money for it. What is not in doubt is that the Wynn family regarded provision for education as particularly worthwhile.

The Gwydir estates were not a creation of the Tudor period; the Margam estates in Glamorgan were. We can follow the fortunes of the Mansel family in the sixteenth century to see how an estate was built up and how its owners acquired increasing influence in the politics and government of their county. The story begins long before 1500. Richard Mansel, born about 1310, started the long process of expanding the family fortunes. His son, Sir Hugh Mansel, married Isabella, daughter of Sir John Penrice; through her inheritance, the Mansels became owners of Oxwich and Penrice Castles in Gower. From then on, the extent of their estates established the Mansels as a family of some consequence. But in 1464 came the disaster of having their lands confiscated after Mansel plots against the Yorkists in the 'Wars of the Roses'. Fortunately for the family, Henry Tudor won the battle of Bosworth and immediately he became king the estates were restored.

However, it was as a result of the career of Sir Rhys Mansel in the first half of the sixteenth century that the family resources grew. He became well known to Henry VIII's government as a result of his important role in the wars in Ireland in the 1530s. This put him in a particularly advantageous position at the time of the dissolution of the monasteries, when large amounts of land in Glamorgan were being sold. Of all the Welsh gentry, Sir Rhys probably profited most from the dissolution. Over six years he bought most of the lands of the former Margam Abbey for the large sum of £2,482 13s. 1d. paid in four instalments. This purchase meant more than the possession of one of the larger estates in south Wales. It provided the Mansel family with a building — the old abbey — which could be converted into one of the most impressive manor houses in the country and it set the seal on their social position. The purchase of Margam was one indication of the importance of the Mansels. Parallel with economic progress went the accumulation of offices. In the 1530s Sir Rhys was a member of the Council of Wales and the Marches, a J.P. and, in 1536, chamberlain of Chester. In the 1540s he was even more distinguished by his service to the army and navy in the war against Scotland. His career reached its peak in 1553 when, as well as being sheriff of Glamorgan for the second time, he was appointed chamberlain and chancellor of south Wales and of the counties of Carmarthenshire and Cardiganshire, the most important office in south Wales. His son, Edward, was much less gifted than his father but the standing of the family in the county was secure. In Elizabeth's reign, Sir Edward Mansel held office as sheriff and J.P.; he was head of one of the six or so most important families in Glamorgan, and was a man of considerable power in the government of the county.

The heads of families like those of Owen, Vaughan, Stradling, Wynn and Mansel played a vital role in the government of their counties in the Elizabethan period. Many of the gentry were not rich by English standards but they were powerful men in their counties. Some, like Rhys Mansel, were both rich and of national standing. Such men held office at the highest level in the provinces. They occasionally served as M.P. for county or borough; when the arduous post of deputy-lieutenant became the most important in county administration in Elizabeth's reign, it was the most important county gentlemen who filled it. The creation of the lieutenancy meant a decline in the importance of the office of sheriff, but the holder still had status and influence and the more important families in each county filled it on many occasions. The range of families providing J.P.s was wider still. Nevertheless, the backbone of the commission, once again, was that group of families whose names are so prominent at all levels of government. Families such as the Mansels and Wynns were virtually permanent members of the commission of the peace. It is only when we arrive at the humbler levels of local government — the level of high constables of the hundreds and petty constables of the parishes who took their orders from the J.P.s — that the holders are generally of humbler origin.

Chapter III

Institutions of Government

1. *Parliament*

The importance of influence, patronage and intrigue in Elizabethan government is well known. In a previous chapter it was stressed that the relationship between Court and county, aristocracy and gentry, was a complex one which worked through a system of power bases and family relationships. Gentry society was often ordered by family ties, loyalty to patrons and wider allegiances. But the politics of influence was played out within a framework of established institutions. At the apex of government was the queen and effective power lay largely with her and her closest advisers, men such as William Cecil, Lord Burleigh. Nevertheless, it was parliament which was responsible for the legal framework within which the gentry worked.

Gentlemen had some hand in ordering that framework through their membership of the Commons. As a result of the act of Union, Wales had a knight to represent every shire and a burgess to represent every borough which was a shire town. There were exceptions: the county of Monmouth was granted two members and no burgess was to sit for Merioneth. In 1542 Haverfordwest was made a county and therefore became entitled to its own member. Representation provided an ideal opportunity for the gentry, because membership of the Commons conferred considerable prestige. Hence, despite the expense involved and the arduous journey to London, Welshmen went to great lengths to get themselves elected to parliament, and, as we saw from the story of the Denbighshire elec-

[I] tion, all kinds of chicanery were possible, particularly because voting was open. However, contested elections were the exception rather than the rule. The gentry had a virtual monopoly of the county seats and were sometimes returned as borough representatives, too, as when William Maurice represented Beaumaris in 1601.

However, the attractions of a seat in parliament lay much more in the influence and patronage which it gave gentlemen in their native counties than in any ability to influence the national framework of government. In fact, the impact of Welsh M.P.s at Westminster — indeed, the whole extent of their participation in national government — was disappointingly small. They made regular requests for leave of absence and were not the most regular attenders in the Commons. This apathetic attitude of the Welsh members is illustrated by the fact that they did not play an effective part in law-making in the period up to 1570. There is only one clear case of a Welsh member being given responsibility for a Welsh bill and that was when Sir Edward Carne of Ewenny, M.P. for Glamorgan, was entrusted with a bill for 'the true making of Welsh friezes'. From about 1570 Welsh M.P.s were more closely involved in legislation, even if at a rather parochial level. Bills were handed over to committees of M.P.s and many Welshmen participated in these during Elizabeth's later parliaments. In 1597, for example, all the Welsh members sat on the committees dealing with the Newport and Caerleon Bridges bill and the bill for the inclusion of the lordship of Llandovery in the county of Carmarthen. These were not matters of national importance, but they do show Welsh members playing a positive part in parliament. Individual Welsh members also sat on committees dealing with more important issues. Sir John Perrot of Pembrokeshire was particularly active following his return for Haverfordwest in 1588-89. He sat on a number of committees, taking charge of a bill in one of them, and he introduced a bill concerned with embezzlement of Crown armour and armaments.

2. *The Privy Council*

Despite the increasing importance of parliament, it sat infrequently and for short sessions, so that the day-to-day administration of the country was carried on at national level by the queen's ministers and the Privy Council in London. The Privy Council made an impact on the lives of the Welsh gentry in two ways. Firstly, it made constant demands on them in their role as county officials. Secondly, on numerous occasions in Elizabeth's reign, it was forced to intervene when gentry rivalries or misdemeanours reached the stage where they began to threaten effective government.

Much of the work of the Privy Council lay in ensuring that the laws of the realm were put into practice in the counties, that the defence of the country was adequate, that there was a sufficient supply of manpower and arms in case of foreign invasion, that the shoreline of the coastal counties was protected. It relied entirely on officials in the counties to implement its orders. So, in Wales, the impact of Privy Council government was felt [2] through the activities of county officials — the deputy lieutenant, sheriff and J.P.s. The Privy Council, then, was the chief instrument of government in the country, advising the monarch on all aspects of policy and assuming responsibility for seeing that policy was implemented. The size of the Privy Council in Elizabeth's reign varied between nine and twenty-nine, significantly fewer than in previous Tudor reigns; the average attendance tended to be no more than eleven. The Council included the most influential men in the kingdom, but this is not to say that they were necessarily great aristocrats. In the early years of Elizabeth's reign, it is true, the Council contained possibly six great lords out of twenty, including the earl of Pembroke. He was lord of Glamorgan, the largest landowner in the county and a man of great influence in Wales. In fact, his career provides us with one of the great success stories of Tudor Wales.

William Herbert first became well known at Court through the influence of the earl of Worcester and from that time onwards his rise was rapid. He accumulated large estates in England and Wales. After the dissolution of the monasteries he bought his Wilton estate in Wiltshire and he also bought up various lordships in Monmouthshire. He became a Privy councillor in 1547, master of the king's horse in 1548-52, and knight of the garter in 1548. After helping to suppress the Western

Rising in 1549, he became earl of Pembroke in 1551. It was he who led the forces which put down Wyatt's rebellion in 1554; in 1556 he was made governor of Calais and in 1557 commanded the English expedition to France. He was made lord steward of Elizabeth's household in 1568. He died in 1570 and was buried in St. Paul's Cathedral. Such, in brief outline, is the career of a Welshman who spoke Welsh more fluently than English, who owned land in numerous counties, who was a diplomat and soldier and who, particularly in Edward VI's reign, was one of the most influential men in the kingdom. He was, however, very much a member of the new aristocracy of the Tudors, unlike some of the other magnates of Elizabeth's Council.

The most important function of the Privy Council was to advise the queen, but its impact on the counties of Wales resulted from its role as the chief administrative and executive body in the country. Again, as Elizabeth's reign proceeded, the amount of local government work which had to be supervised, as well as the increase in the number of private petitions sent to the Council, was reflected in the number of times it met — three times a week in the earlier part of the reign and almost every day by the 1590s. Moreover, a change was taking place in the composition of the Council in that it became a much more professional body of advisers and administrators, with the number of great lords down to one by the end of the reign.

The affair of the famous cross in the ash tree at St. Donat's has already provided one example of how the Privy Council intervened in a matter of particular sensitivity. This kind of intervention in gentry society had to be finely judged. Men like Stradling were essential to the good government which it was the Privy Council's concern to provide. On the other hand, his devotion to the Catholic cause could become, as on this occasion, not only an impediment to effective local government but a matter of national importance. This episode gives ample indication of the power of the Privy Council. Its orders, carried by one of the forty or so messengers at its disposal, were brought to local officials, who were detailed to carry out an investigation. Stradling was summoned to London, brought before the councillors in person and eventually imprisoned in the Tower of London. One of the conditions of his release, it may be remembered, was that he was bound to appear before the Council at twelve days' warning.

This provides only one example of the way in which the Council kept a close eye on the Welsh gentry. Justice — often abuse of justice particularly when important local gentry were involved — was among its major preoccupations. In the first year of Elizabeth's reign the Council intervened in a case which involved two very important gentry families. The complex background to this story will emerge later and, at this stage, it is sufficient to say that there had been a riot at Oxwich in Gower which involved Sir George Herbert of Swansea and Edward, the son of Sir Rhys Mansel of Margam. The cause of the dispute was that a ship had gone aground near Oxwich bay and its cargo had been taken away by Sir Rhys's men. Sir George Herbert objected that, as vice-admiral, he was entitled to take custody of wrecked ships and their cargo. Sir George's men and those of Edward Mansel eventually confronted each other outside the Oxwich manor house of the Mansels and an aged relative, Ann Mansel, was accidentally killed by a stone. Eventually, a trial for murder came before the court of Star Chamber, but the Privy Council was less concerned with the judicial aspects of the case on this occasion than with the obviously deteriorating relations between two such important families. Their co-operation with each other was vital if there was to be effective government in west Glamorgan. Once the Privy Council was informed of the riot, Sir George Herbert was summoned immediately to London to give an account of it. The Privy Council wrote at the same time to the Council in the Marches requesting an investigation and the arrest of the offenders. Sir George Herbert himself travelled to London immediately and was ordered not to leave the capital. He appeared before the Privy Council three times in quick succession. Subsequently, it intervened directly and sent detailed instructions to the Council in the Marches as to how the case should be investigated; at a later stage it even determined the level of compensation to be paid by Sir George Herbert to the Mansels. It finally demonstrated just how wide was its supervision of local affairs by attempting to bring about a reconciliation between these two powerful foes. Good relations between them were vital and four members of the Council, including the lord treasurer, were detailed to try to settle the dispute amicably, although it was not long before the Mansels and the Herberts clashed again.

Confrontations between gentlemen in the counties, with grave consequences for good government, were always treated seriously by the Privy Council. Other major problems which cropped up regularly involved officials of the counties, such as J.P.s and sheriffs, not doing their work competently; piracy and smuggling, of which there was a great deal around the Welsh coasts in Elizabeth's reign; and military affairs. Since local officials, particularly the local gentry who were deputy lieutenants, were responsible for providing men for the army, having them trained and providing them with armour (which was generally kept in gentry houses), it is obvious that the Council would be desperately concerned that this aspect of local administration should be competently carried out, particularly at times of crisis such as the 1570s and 1580s. This was especially so in south Wales because Milford Haven was regarded as vulnerable, and Holyhead in north Wales was another obvious landing place. Religion provided another perpetual problem for the Privy Council. Local gentry were often detailed to look for Catholic priests active in the locality, as was Sir Thomas Mansel of Margam, who was ordered in 1596 to search for two Catholic priests reputed to be at the house of a recusant family in the county. It is small wonder, given the scope of this supervision in virtually all aspects of local government and justice and the frequency of its intervention, that the Privy Council was in daily session by the end of Elizabeth's reign.

3. *The Westminster Courts: Star Chamber, Chancery, Requests and Exchequer.*

The second half of the sixteenth century saw the strengthening of links between Wales and some of the Westminster courts. These may be divided into the equity and prerogative courts of

Star Chamber, Chancery and Requests; and the ancient common law courts of Exchequer, King's Bench and Common Pleas. One of the important distinctions between the two types of court was that the former could judge cases on grounds of equity and thus establish precedents, while the latter could judge only on precedent. However, one of the vital differences between the administration of justice in England and Wales was that the act of Union had set up a distinctive judicial system for Wales. Twelve of the Welsh counties (Monmouthshire was excluded) were grouped into four circuits. The justice of each circuit was to hold great sessions in each county twice every year. These courts, which we will investigate in a later chapter, fulfilled the functions of the courts of King's Bench and Common Pleas and they remained a distinctive feature of Welsh justice until the nineteenth century. The officials and lawyers of the common law courts at Westminster resented this aspect of Welsh autonomy, particularly as great sessions seem to have acquired an all-important equity jurisdiction early on in their history. This fact did not mean that no Welsh cases were taken to the equity and prerogative courts at Westminster. On the contrary, the Westminster courts had a considerable impact on the lives of the Welsh gentry, though less in their offical capacity than as private individuals. Between them the courts had jurisdiction over a whole range of cases, from murder and other violent crimes to the settlement of title to land and financial matters. The official demands they made on the gentry were not excessive and mainly involved the collection of evidence. Star Chamber, in particular, relied on the gentry (particularly as J.P.s) to take evidence in the form of depositions from witnesses. However, as individuals, most gentlemen were involved at one time or another with the London courts. These courts offered an opportunity to settle disputes peacefully and there can be little doubt that they helped to foster a greater respect for the law, though the degree to which they exercised this influence is a matter of dispute among historians. They also imposed constraints on the gentry because these were important national courts. One of the themes of gentry participation in government is that most gentlemen were tempted on occasion

Henry Herbert, Second Earl of Pembroke.
Source: National Museum of Wales.

Vera effigies Clariss. Do.ni Iohañis Wynn de Gwedúr in
Com Carnarvon Equitis et Baronetti &c.
Obijt primo die Martij 1626. Ætat: 73.

Honoris ipfius caufa   Ro vaughan fcut   Profeque D.D:

Sir John Wynn of Gwydir.
Source: The National Library of Wales.

Mansel Family Tombs in Margam Abbey Church.
Source: Royal Commission on Ancient Monuments.

Carew Castle, Pembrokeshire, granted to Sir John Perrot in 1554.
Source: Royal Commission on Ancient Monuments in Wales and Monmouthshire.

St. Donat's Castle, home of the Stradlings.
Source: H. Tempest, Cardiff Ltd.

Gwydir, Caernarvonshire. Home of the Wynns.
Source: Royal Commission of Ancient Monuments in Wales and Monmouthshire.

Sir Thomas Stradling's complaint to the Privy Council accusing William Herbert of Cogan Pill of illegal exactions while mustering men on behalf of the Earl of Pembroke.

Source: Public Record Office. STA CHA 4/4/29.

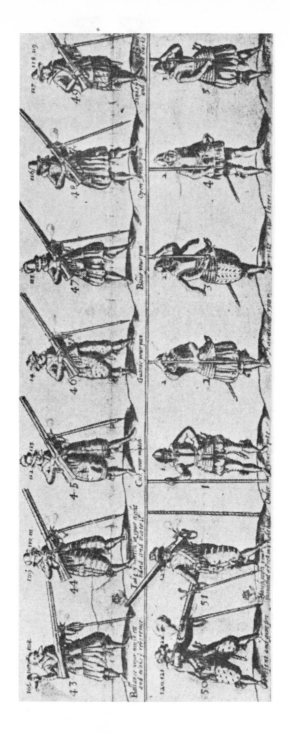

Drill movements with musket and pike.
Source: The British Museum.

to abuse their privileges of wealth, position and office to further their own interests. It was the Westminster courts, as we shall see, that provided the most satisfactory machinery for containing such abuses.

Star Chamber heard its cases in public, meeting on Wednesdays and Fridays from 9 o'clock to 11 o'clock in the morning; its great attraction for suitors was, firstly, its strength (since it was basically the Privy Council sitting as a court) and, secondly, its speed. It dealt with both public and private cases, the former as a result of bills of complaint brought by the attorney-general and the latter on receipt of bills from private attorneys. One private bill was brought in 1595 by the two bailiffs of Cardiff, Nicholas Hawkins and Charles Froude, against Sir William Herbert and Nicholas Herbert. This spectacular case had started in February 1595, after a disturbance at the house of a wine-merchant in Cardiff. The trouble was almost certainly caused by servants of Sir William and Nicholas Herbert and they were taken to the town hall to be questioned by the bailiffs, though the officials were forced to release them when more of the Herbert retainers turned up in violent mood. The following day the rioters were arrested, only to be forcibly released by an armed band of Nicholas Herbert's men. They also attacked one of the bailiffs, who was sufficiently badly hurt to have to be carried home. The released prisoners were taken back to Sir William Herbert's house, where the irons which had bound them were hammered off.

Some three weeks later one of the original rioters, Llywelyn David, died of wounds received in the fight. The Herberts were determined not to let the matter of this 'murder' rest there, and a series of events followed which were bizarre even in the context of Tudor justice. The sheriff, whose genius for corruption we shall look at more closely later, happened to be a cousin of the Herberts and he demanded an inquest on Llywelyn David. It was the sheriff's responsibility to produce a jury to serve on the inquest and he made certain that the jury was picked from a list of men favourable to the Herberts. In fact it contained a number of Herbert relations. A special court was then held in Cardiff, with Sir William Herbert himself on the bench; a bill of riot was brought against the townsmen of Cardiff. The townsmen naturally protested at the fact that the proceedings were not in public, but it was to no avail. Sir William Herbert personally instructed the witnesses in what they were to say in full view of the jury and the jury promptly brought in a verdict against the townsmen. A bill of riot brought by the townsmen against Sir William Herbert's men was quickly rejected.

It is at this point in the story that the court of Star Chamber becomes crucial. Important, influential gentry families, themselves occupying positions of authority and trust in local government, had distorted the instruments of justice in order to perpetrate a profound injustice and obtain a false verdict. It was only a court such as Star Chamber, with its greater authority, that could discipline such powerful families as the Herberts. Star Chamber provided a means of redress for the bailiffs of Cardiff. They brought a bill against the Herberts and their servants, and Star Chamber found the Herberts guilty. Sir William and Nicholas were committed to the Fleet prison. The other chief rioters were to be put in the pillory on two occasions, with papers in their hands showing their offences; in addition, they were to pay a fine of £200 apiece. Sir William Herbert was fined 1,000 marks and Nicholas Herbert £500. Both were to pay £200 damages to Hawkins and Froude. It is noteworthy that while Nicholas Herbert was no longer to be a J.P., Sir William Herbert continued to serve as a member of the Council in the Marches.

The court of Star Chamber, then, had succeeded in obtaining justice for the weaker side on this occasion, as on many others. Powerful gentlemen had initially taken advantage of their role as law enforcers to become law breakers, but they had found that they could not break the law with impunity. The court of Star Chamber could not be ignored even by the most important gentry in Wales.

In less spectacular fashion, the other important London courts played their part in administration and justice in Wales. The court of Chancery was an important institution administering civil law. Not only could it cope with cases raising new legal issues which the more rigid common law courts could not deal with, but it was generally more flexible in its procedures. It was hampered later on in the century by the ever-increasing demands made on it as both a court of justice and an administrative body. The court of Requests was equally popular with Welshmen, and both courts dealt with a variety of cases — land disputes, disputes over rents, legacies, loans, tithes, refusal to pass on deeds, marriage settlements — in fact, a vast range of financial matters. The court of Exchequer was a similar body. Originally it had dealt with cases concerning royal revenue, but by Elizabeth's reign, it was giving judgement in cases between individuals and, like Chancery, was attractive to suitors because of its greater speed. The number of suits brought to the Exchequer from Wales and the border counties of Herefordshire and Shropshire in Elizabeth's reign was 667. The largest number of suits by far came from Denbighshire (104), the fewest from Radnor (20). These cases were concerned mainly with debts owing to the monarch or the recovery of lands, goods or other profits owing to the Crown. The court itself was held in the Exchequer Chamber at Westminster before the lord treasurer, the chancellor of the Exchequer, the chief baron and three barons of the Exchequer. The number of cases coming from Wales was surprisingly large, considering the facilities available in the Council in the Marches and, indeed, in the powerful court of great sessions. It has been argued that the reason for this was that litigants felt that they could not obtain justice in Wales itself because of local influence exerted by opponents, particularly in packing juries with their own sympathisers; and there is certainly some truth in this.

A case which demonstrates just how complex the working of the law could be in Elizabeth's reign involved two north Wales families, those of William Maurice and Hugh Lloyd. The dispute lasted from 1578 until 1590, and during that period Hugh Lloyd brought two actions against William Maurice, one in the Exchequer, the other in the Council in the Marches; Maurice countered with actions in both Exchequer and Star Chamber. Later, Lloyd took the case to the consistory court of the bishop of Bangor and, yet again, to the court of Exchequer.

The dispute itself was over the premises of the collegiate church of Holyhead and four other churches and chapels. Maurice claimed that the lease of these premises, originally granted by Edward VI to William Lewis, had been inherited by his wife, but that Hugh Lloyd had made malicious attempts to gain two new leases which would cancel the old. After the first hearings in the Exchequer and the Council in the Marches, Hugh Lloyd had been granted possession of three of the chapels and William Maurice was to have the fourth. Both parties entered into a bond of £300 to observe the order. Hugh Lloyd then managed to get an Exchequer order against Maurice and brought an action of debt against him, alleging that he had not obeyed the order of the Council in the Marches that he leave the premises. Maurice countered this by taking the matter back to the Council in the Marches, which ordered the bond to be cancelled. So, the endless litigation over land which took up so much of the gentry's time, interest and energy is illustrated here in a typical case. So often were titles to land unwritten, or at least difficult to prove from the records, that there were innumerable opportunities for grievances such as this to arise and then to be shuttled backwards and forwards between the various courts empowered to deal with financial and property disputes.

4. *The Council in the Marches*

The organ of government with which the Welsh gentry were most closely involved as local officials was the Council in the Marches. It fulfilled the sometimes paradoxical role of providing them with a great deal of routine administration and at the same time of trying to ensure that they carried out their responsibilities effectively.

In the action between Lloyd and Maurice which we looked at [3] in the previous section, the Council loomed large as a court. As such it had a wide jurisdiction not only over civil matters but also over criminal cases. This was coupled with comprehensive powers in both the maintenance of law and order and the general administration of Wales. The origins of the Council are to be found in the fifteenth century, but it was only with the act of Union that it was set up on a statutory basis. As a result, it developed rapidly both as a court of law and as an administrative body. As a court it had jurisdiction over the Welsh counties, together with Herefordshire, Gloucestershire, Worcestershire, Shropshire and, until 1569, Cheshire. It had the widest powers and could try cases of murder and treason, though most of its time was taken up with lesser criminal and civil cases.

4   As an administrative body its powers were just as extensive. Its most important concerns were to preserve law and order, supervise local officials, cater for the defence of the country, supervise and train men for military service, look after the storage and condition of armour, and try to control recusancy. These functions, of course, were exactly those which most concerned the Privy Council, and it is worth looking briefly at the relationship between the two. The Privy Council normally acted as supervisor of the Council in the Marches, as of the other great courts in the country. Not that the Privy Council always acted through the Council in the Marches, because there are numerous instances of direct intervention by the Privy Council in Welsh affairs; but, in general, the Council in the Marches acted as its agent in Wales. The Privy Council referred cases to the Council in the Marches and often intervened in the conduct of specific cases, advised on punishments and the granting of bail, and provided a back-up authority for those who took the Council in the Marches too lightly. In fact, there was virtually no aspect of the work of the Council in the Marches which was not at some point subject to the detailed supervision of Westminster. The general climate of the relationship was healthy enough, and the Privy Council was almost invariably prepared to delegate cases to the Welsh Council.

Again, it is obvious that the functions of the Council in the Marches overlapped, to some extent, those of Star Chamber. Many cases went to both courts, since it was common practice in the Elizabethan period for defendants in one court to bring actions against their opponents in another. It does seem, though, that on some occasions the Council in the Marches was incapable of withstanding the considerable power of the more important Welsh gentry, and such cases had to be dealt with in Star Chamber.

There was a similar overlap between the Council in the Marches and the court of Exchequer in cases involving disputes over Crown lands, debts and royal revenue. Here, again, many cases were heard in both courts, as we have seen in the protracted battle between William Maurice and Hugh Lloyd. It was not that the Council in the Marches was any less efficient than the London courts, but that, to quote Penry Williams, 'in an age of increasing litigation, suitors were ready to try any court that would hear their cases'. The Exchequer was the superior court, as the case involving the son of Sir Richard Bulkeley of Beaumaris illustrates. Sir Richard accused his stepmother of murdering his father, but she was aquitted. Bulkeley then claimed the manor of Anglesey from his stepmother, who took the case to the Council in the Marches; the court of Exchequer intervened and requested the Welsh court not to hear the case since the manor was Crown land. After some hesitation, the Council in the Marches agreed to the request.

There were comparatively few Welshmen on the Council in the Marches. Those who did become members were generally brought in late in Elizabeth's reign and were wealthy and well established gentry. Sir William Herbert of Swansea, who was made a member in 1590 and featured so notoriously in the Cardiff riot of 1595, belonged to an important branch of the earl of Pembroke's family. Sir Thomas Mansel, who became a member in the last year of Elizabeth's reign, was also the head of a particularly influential family in south Wales and played a prominent part in local government as deputy-lieutenant and in parliament as M.P. for Glamorgan. Sir John Perrot of Haverfordwest joined the Council in 1574, and was vice-admiral of south Wales and three times M.P. There was Ellis Price of Denbighshire, an eminent lawyer who was admitted to the Council in 1560; Richard Price of Gogerddan in Cardiganshire, deputy lieutenant and six times M.P. for the county; Sir Richard Trevor of Denbighshire, who became a councillor in 1601. Membership of the Council was the preserve of the élite among the gentry.

5   On the other hand, the work of the Council involved the participation of local officials at all levels and in this way affected greater numbers of gentlemen. It is this administrative work of the Council that we know best since the detailed records of its work as a court no longer survive. The Council was partly responsible for selecting local officials from among the gentry. It was on these officials, of course, that the success of the Council's work depended. Inevitably the Council in the Marches was in closer touch with the county gentry than was the central government, and it played an important part in selecting deputy-lieutenants, sheriffs and justices of the peace. However, its influence could often be counteracted by that of an earl of Essex in south Wales or by an earl of Leicester in north Wales, who was able to get a number of his henchmen placed on the commisson of the peace. The Council was also responsible for compiling short lists of possible sheriffs for each county and the lord president's voice was generally decisive in the final appointment. Here again, the great magnates of the realm were anxious to use their influence. Deputy-lieutenants were normally appointed on the advice of the lord president, who was lord lieutenant for all Wales. Every aspect of local administration in which these officials were involved came under the aegis of the Council in the Marches in one form or an other. The comprehensive supervisory responsibilities of this Council are readily illustrated from documents produced during the last five years of Sir Henry Sidney's presidency. His term of office is generally regarded as the high point of the Council's existence, though by the 1580s rivalries within the Council (especially between the Leicester group led by Sidney himself and the opposing faction of Croft and Whitgift) were having a detrimental effect. These rivalries had their counterpart in rivalries between Council officials. There were financial problems too. Nevertheless, at a crucial time in England's history, culminating in the sailing of the Armada two years after Sidney's death, the Council was doing sterling work, particularly in matters of defence and the maintenance of law and order.

January 1584 saw an important letter from the Privy Council

which reflected national concern at the possibility of the Welsh coast being invaded by foreign troops. This letter, in fact, refers specifically to Anglesey. Speaking of 'these dangerous times', the Privy Council asked that the muster-masters in the county assemble the trained men of the island and ensure that they were in a state of readiness for any emergency. Musters were to be taken also in the neighbouring counties of Merioneth and Caernarvon. The J.P.s and important gentlemen of the three counties were to join together to undertake the musters and make returns of how many men were available in each county.

The flexibility of the relationship between the Council in the Marches and the Privy Council is well illustrated by a development in May 1584. In January the Council in the Marches had been ordered to organise musters. Now it was being informed by the Privy Council that a more professional assessment of men and armour in the north-west was needed and Richard Gwynne of Conway was recommended as the man for the job. The Council in the Marches was to arrange payment for him. A copy of Richard Gwynne's instructions from the Privy Council was attached. The orders were detailed and instructed Gwynne to meet the sheriff, the commissioner for musters, and all the local gentry to assess the forces available and advise them on how best the training and organisation of the trained bands could be accomplished. What is particularly interesting about these instructions from a major organ of national government is that so little was left to chance. The commissioners for musters, who, as local gentry, would have had experience of local administration, were to provide Gwynne with a list of all men and weapons available. He was then to divide the men into bands of two hundred. The main concern was to be the training of the 'shot' (the men who had charge of the cannon), a process which took two months. Gwynne was to spend two days of each week with the 'shot' of each division, and two days with the pikemen, bowmen and billmen, whose training was much easier. Unskilled bowmen, in particular, had to be weeded out and replaced before a second review took place. There were detailed instructions, too, on how the training was to be carried out. A final point, which must be borne in mind, is that the local gentry played a vital role in all this, not only as commissioners for musters but as commanders, or captains, responsible for the weekly training. What mattered was not that they should be skilled soldiers, but that they should be gentlemen. And where the captain is unskilful, being as we wish the eldest son of a principal gentleman, . . . then may you cause some man skilful in martial profession inhabiting thereabout to assist him.'

A document dated 10 December 1585 serves as a reminder that one of the recurring problems in Elizabethan Wales was that of violence and disorder. It seems partly a case of the cat being away, since Lord President Sidney had been absent from Ludlow for two years. Sidney revealed how outraged he was that, despite all the offences of fighting and rioting, no complaints were being made to him by local sheriffs and J.P.s — an explicit statement of how negligent the county gentry could be. The upshot was that sheriffs and other officers of the shires were to notify the lord president of all recent offences which had not yet been punished and to make strenuous efforts to catch the people involved.

The Council in the Marches made constant attempts to fulfil its role as the supervisor of an efficient system of local administration and justice. The degree of success varied, of course, but to this end it was constantly in touch with the county gentry in their official capacity, particularly over such matters as defence and law and order. Without their co-operation with the Council and the national organs of government, administration of government and justice in the counties could not succeed.

5. *The Great Sessions*

As J.P.s the gentry were equally vital in the administration of the court of great sessions. For information on these courts we can turn to George Owen. As we have seen, Owen was a successful Pembrokeshire gentleman who shared all the prejudices of his class. He was particularly committed to the system of government inaugurated by the act of Union. We must not therefore expect him to pay too much attention to the faults of that system; but a contemporary verdict is still invaluable. Owen records that great sessions were to be held every six months in each county by a justice of assize responsible for a circuit of three counties. Accompanying the justice on his circuit was a protonotary who was responsible for organising and recording the procedures of the court. The range of cases with which the justices dealt was large. George Owen's list includes murder, robbery, theft, rio , extortion and corruption of juries. Owen was flattering about not only the breadth of the court's jurisdiction but also the great care with which cases were heard and the skill of the justices. In fact, when it comes to finding fault with the system, his major complaint was that the sessions were held at particularly busy times of the year, either at sowing or harvest time.

Those of the gentry who were J.P.s played a vital part in the working of the great sessions in numerous ways. After a crime had been committed and the criminal arrested, he was brought before a J.P., who would spend up to two days questioning both him and the witnesses to the crime. The justice then had to ensure that the prisoner turned up at the sessions to answer charges against him and that prosecutors and witnesses were also available at the right time. The case then went through a preliminary enquiry in front of a grand jury, whose function was to present the case for trial, and then a petty jury of twelve, who had to be unanimous in their verdict. One weakness of this system which George Owen highlighted was that after the justices had finished their original examination they washed their hands of the case and, as a result, many cases in which a compromise agreement had already been reached between the two sides were brought to the great sessions quite unnecessarily and wasted valuable time.

J.P.s were involved in other ways in the great sessions, either as members of first or second inquests, or, indeed, in following their own cases as defendants or complainants. Since these courts had extensive powers, many cases involving gentlemen were tried there, though important and serious breaches of the law, particularly if corrupt practices were involved, tended to go to the London courts of Star Chamber or Chancery. Again, cases could go to a number of different courts at various stages. But one thing is clear. The courts of great sessions were, in sixteenth-century terms, efficient and objective; they were relatively cheap and near at hand, were convened regularly and became an increasingly significant instrument of justice as Elizabeth's reign ran its course.

Chapter IV

County Servants

National and provincial institutions of government provided executive opportunities for few of the Welsh gentlemen. The framework within which these gentlemen worked and the constraints upon them were decided by others. Nevertheless, the national organs of government and justice could only function with the co-operation of county officials. It was this that provided the gentry with the opportunity of playing an important part in the government of Wales.

In England the most important local officials in terms of power and social rank were the lords lieutenant. The office was created after the Reformation as a military safeguard against possible rebellion and disturbance. In the first half of Elizabeth's reign, lords lieutenant were not appointed regularly, though in some cases they changed annually. They were appointed for each county, and from the 1580s onwards allowed to stay at their posts for life. This was a particularly important development because many of the lords lieutenant were occupied in government at national level, and as a result the office of deputy-lieutenant came into being.

In Wales the situation was different. There was only one lord lieutenant and in Elizabeth's reign he was invariably the president of the Council in the Marches. Even when no lord lieutenant was specifically appointed, the president in fact carried out his duties. Deputy-lieutenants were necessary in Wales not so much because of the life appointment of lords lieutenant and heavy military duties (as in England), but because the area under the lord lieutenant's control was so large. According to Penry Williams, 'From early in the reign, the Council delegated the tasks of mustering, equipping and levying the county militias to local commissioners in each shire. After Pembroke's appointment in 1586 (as Lord President of the Council in the Marches), deputy-lieutenants were nominated in every shire . . .'

By the second half of Elizabeth's reign, the lord lieutenant's main task was to supervise the work of his deputy-lieutenants, after he had given his advice on who should be appointed. The queen, or her ministers, could nominate deputies without asking for the opinion of the lord lieutenant but this was not normal. There was no fixed number of deputies, though each served only one county. None of the Welsh counties had as many as the six deputies serving in Devon in the 1580s, but most of them had two.

As with all local officials under the Tudors, the deputy-lieutenant had more than enough work to occupy him. His job was primarily a military one, and in many of the Welsh counties this was of great importance, as urgent communications from the Council in the Marches and the Privy Council show. In the first place, there was always the possibility of invasion through one of the Welsh ports, particularly Milford Haven and Holyhead. Second, there was the allied problem of Ireland which could serve either as a base for Spanish invasion or as a theatre of war itself. One obvious route to England lay through the Welsh ports, and the residents of the south-western and north-western counties of Wales were just as conscious of this as was the central government. The deputy-lieutenants of these shires had a special responsibility to see that the county militia was up to scratch in its numbers, training and weapons. Mustering, the term used for assembling, inspecting and training troops, was the basic duty of the deputy-lieutenant, and all the details of the fit men under training and their weapons were to be recorded in muster books which could be — and often were — inspected by the Privy Council. In the days before the advent of the deputy-lieutenant, mustering was done by special commissioners appointed by the queen, although two paid officials, a muster master and a provost marshal, helped in the work; the former carried out a detailed inspection of men, horses and armour, while the latter looked after discipline. Deputy-lieutenants had other responsibilities. When the Crown was raising loans in the counties, they had to provide lists of men of means and an estimate of how much each might be able to pay. They also had the problem of supervising recusants.

None of the work of a deputy-lieutenant in Wales was easy. More than this, he was not likely to be a popular figure, particularly in the later years of Elizabeth's reign. It was difficult to assemble good men for musters when they were required only for service in their counties; when they were needed for service abroad it became almost impossible. And service abroad was becoming more of a necessity, whether in the Netherlands or, for Welshmen, in Ireland; as many as two thousand were required for service across St. George's Channel by 1600. It is little wonder that complaints from commanders about the quality of troops became more and more frequent.

It might be thought that any office which carried such responsibilities and problems would not be much sought after, but this was not the case. There are two main reasons why important gentry families competed for the deputy-lieutenancy. One is the prestige which went with the office, the most important in the pyramid of county administration. Among the deputy-lieutenants were such eminent gentry as William Maurice of Clenennau, Sir John Wynn of Gwydir, Sir William Herbert of Swansea, Sir Richard Trevor in Denbighshire, and Sir Thomas Jones in Carmarthenshire. Secondly, there is no doubt that the deputy-lieutenant wielded considerable influence. He was in a strong position to deal with other local officials, such as J.P.s, and he could excuse men from military service or condone their absence from musters. For the more unscrupulous there was always the opportunity to make illegal profits out of the office, though this was not common. The worst instance of corruption at this level involved Cadwaladr Price of Merioneth. He was appointed deputy-lieutenant and sheriff in Merionethshire purely through the patronage of the earl of Pembroke, who was lord president. In 1598, nine years after his appointment, Price and his fellow deputy, John Lewis Owen, were accused in Star Chamber of embezzling armour valued at £1,000, of taxing people illegally, putting them in prison when they refused to pay and of making a profit out of musters. It seems certain that these accusations were correct, particularly since the local moderates said that Owen depended on the deputy-lieutenancy for a living. This amounted to direct evidence of corruption, since lieutenants, like other local officials, were unpaid. Certainly the court of Star Chamber was in no doubt. The two deputy-lieutenants were dismissed from office and outlawed.

It is usual to think of the influence of the sheriff of the county declining as that of the deputy-lieutenant increased. To some extent this is true. The influence which the sheriff had earlier exercised in military matters was lost. He was not, in the Elizabethan period, the chief official of the county, but nevertheless he was an important figure. Well into the reign, the sheriffs of each county were detailed to take musters. Even without his military responsibilities the sheriff had more than enough work to do, helped only by a small staff: a county gaoler, sheriff's bailiff and hundred bailiff. At meetings of quarter sessions and great sessions he was responsible for providing juries, producing prisoners, levying fines and carrying out sentences. He had to ensure that all royal letters reached their destination safely and that taxes were collected. He served all writs and processes. A significant part of his work is seen at election time: he not only took charge of the county court, where the elections were held, but he also declared and returned the result. The events in Denbighshire (related in the Introduction) indicate the sort of illegal pressure that could be exerted in an open election when a show of hands decided the result.

Mention of the county court serves as a reminder that the sheriff, by the act of 1543, was still responsible for holding a monthly county court and a fortnightly hundred court to hear cases involving an amount less than 40*s*. These courts were held regularly in Elizabeth's reign, but because their records have disappeared it is difficult to assess their importance. It is generally agreed that both courts became progressively less significant as J.P.s assumed an ever greater degree of administrative and judicial responsibility. Nevertheless, the hundred courts, in particular, served a useful function in settling numerous cases of small debt which were a feature of Tudor society. George Owen was critical of these courts but his emphasis was on reform, not abolition.

Historians have concluded that the sheriff's office was a very unpopular one because of the weight of duties and the considerable costs which the sheriff had to meet. These included paying the salary of an under-sheriff and providing hospitality for distinguished visitors to the county. However, there is no indication that the gentry were anxious to avoid holding the office. Certainly most substantial gentlemen served as sheriff of their county and a number did so at regular intervals. There are, perhaps, two main reasons why competition should have been greater in Wales than is generally supposed. First, the accompanying prestige and influence of a still novel office were important not only to the gentry themselves but to their patrons. There is no doubt that the earl of Pembroke was very anxious that as many as possible of the sheriffs should be his allies. Secondly, the influence of the sheriff in matters of law and order and in elections could often be put to profitable use, and cases of corruption illustrate that this was so. Probably the most notorious of Welsh sheriffs, in this respect, was Edward Kemeys, of Cefn Mabli in Glamorgan. [6]

The Kemeyses came from Monmouthshire, and by the fifteenth century were a family of some consequence in Glamorgan, having made good use of that important ladder to prosperity, a wealthy marriage. It was through marriage that the Kemeys connection with Cefn Mabli began, for in the mid-fifteenth century Ieuan Kemeys married the heiress to lands situated there. By the beginning of Elizabeth's reign, the family was well established in Glamorgan, and Edward Kemeys, head of the family for much of the reign, was sheriff of Glamorgan four times. His first period of office was in 1575-76, a time when piracy on the southern coast of Wales was a problem. In particular, John Callice was making a good living by his piracy near the port of Cardiff. There is evidence that he was doing so with the connivance of the Herberts. Among the Herbert allies were two important gentry families, the Lewises of the Van and the Kemeyses. Unfortunately, we do not know exactly what Kemey's links with the pirates were but he was sent for by the judge of Admiralty on 12 January 1576 to answer charges of assisting Callice and other pirates. He did not turn up. A messenger had been sent to Cefn Mabli to summon him but he was not at home. He was also warned by the sheriff, Sir Edward Mansel of Margam. Among those who did turn up at the investigation was John Thomas, a Glamorgan J.P. He was charged with allowing the bail of two pirate suspects, Collins and Court. 'He saith he was not privy thereunto, for one Edward Kemeys used his name therein without his knowledge.' Of course, we cannot be certain that Thomas's accusation was correct and we have no knowledge of any subsequent investigation. Even if it were true, Kemeys had not taken the trouble to turn up to deny it.

Ten years later Kemeys was in office again. This time there were two serious charges of the sheriff's misuse of office. The better documented is that made by David Morgan of Usk, though it must be remembered that only the charge survives, not the court's verdict. David Morgan accused Kemeys of selling offices. Morgan himself was keeper of the gaol in Glamorgan and had appointed as his deputy John Hughes of Cardiff,

> who by the space of three years did hold the same, until now the said Edward Kemeys hath unjustly taken money and bonds of the said John Hughes for the said Gaolership, and afterwards put out . . . John Hughes from that office, and also hath imprisoned him and doth wrongfully detain him in close prison in the said Gaol. And . . . Edward Kemeys hath also sold sundry offices belonging to his said Sheriffship; to one John Andrews the under-sheriffship for 70s.; to Thomas Williams the Clerkship of the county for 70s.; his Bailiffship to Thomas Llewelyn for 8s.; the Bailiwicke of the Hundred of Gibon (Kibbor) and Cardiff to Maurice Howell for 12s; . . .

Then follows a list of the offices of each hundred in Glamorgan, the names of the buyers and the amounts they paid. The total amount which is said to have gone into Kemeys's pocket was the substantial one of £492 6s. 8d.

In 1595 Kemeys was once more sheriff of Glamorgan. Perhaps it was a case of practice making perfect, but in this year Kemeys excelled himself. There were two misdemeanours during the year which led to complaints in the court of Exchequer in 1599 and 1600. The first was from Nicholas Hawkins, bailiff of Cardiff. His story was that Edward Kemeys had asked William Vaughan, a servant, to sell offices in the sheriff's gift. Vaughan had sold the clerkship of the county to William Roberts, who entered into a bond with Kemeys for the purchase price. Parts of the bond were broken and Kemeys began a suit against Roberts. Hawkins stood bail for Roberts. Kemeys, however, bore a grudge against Hawkins who, as the document rightly tells us, had given evidence in Star Chamber against him for serious abuse of office as sheriff. Kemeys therefore forced William Vaughan to sue Hawkins over the matter of the bond. He managed to get a verdict against Roberts, but instead of prosecuting, he had him imprisoned in Cardiff gaol so that he would be unable to meet his bail. After complicated legal in-fighting, Kemeys was in a perfect position to take revenge on Hawkins. He secured writs against Hawkins for failing to produce Roberts and put Hawkins in gaol.

Kemeys also attempted extortion against his deputy-sheriff, William St. John. St. John had entered into a bond, backed by his father Christopher St. John and Thomas Bawdrem, that he would perform his duties as under-sheriff properly. By maintaining that St. John had not been doing his job satisfactorily, Kemeys could blackmail his deputy and, according to St. John, had already been paid £20 with a promise of another £20 in two years. But apparently Kemeys was getting too greedy. He had asked St. John for another £7 which St. John had refused to pay and, as a result, Kemeys started a court case against his deputy, though we have no means of knowing whether the case came to anything.

An incident in which Kemeys played a very unsavoury part

involved a court case in great sessions and elsewhere over the ownership of a sandy area of Merthyr Mawr in Glamorgan. Kemeys's role here was that of jury-rigging. The main opponents in the case were Griffith Williams and Sir Edward Stradling, and Williams was said to have boasted 'to all clients that came to him, that he marvelled much what Sir Edward Stradling meant in thinking to have a jury that should pass against Sir William Herbert'. This claim rings true for one outstanding reason, that Edward Kemeys, as sheriff, was responsible for producing the jury. John Stradling, who wrote an account of the case, reserves some of his most vindictive writing for Kemeys.

> And it fell out so that against the next assizes the Lawyer (Williams) had a sheriff fit for his own humour, one father Edward Kemeys of Cefn Mabli, or of Llanwonno or of the Collegiate Cathedral Church of St. Austins in Bristol, for in each of these places he keepeth his habitation by Turns, he cannot abide to dwell long in one house, fearing to be overmuch frequented with his friends, would god I had time to write a chronicle of this mans doings ... But to let him pass and come again to our argument, he returned such a *decem tales* [reserve jury], [as] never honest man had seen before that time returned ...

He goes on to give an account of just how the jury was made up and how each member was linked with the family of Sir William Herbert, who was the power behind Griffith Williams. Some were related to the Herberts, others were family retainers. All were drawn, in Stradling's words, from 'the remote quarters of the Countie', by which he meant that none came from the area where Stradling influence was strongest.

In February 1595, the infamous Cardiff riot which, it will be recalled, involved the familiar figure of Nicholas Hawkins, one of Cardiff's bailiffs, and Sir William Herbert, provided a suitably dramatic backcloth for more of Edward Kemeys's operations. After the initial riot and the forcible release of the Herbert retainers from the town hall, the central issue was the death of Llywelyn David, one of Herbert's men, who died from injuries received during the fighting. It was here that Kemeys's allegiance to the Herbert cause came in very useful. The first necessity, from the Herbert point of view, was to empanel a jury which would return a favourable verdict at the inquest. This was no problem to a practised operator like Kemeys, as the court of Star Chamber was informed.

> What sinister and indirect courses were taken to lay the death and murder of the said Llywelyn David upon the . . . townsmen [of Cardiff], as the authors and beginners of the said affray and tumult, And the better to effect the same, one Edward Kemeys, then high sheriff of the County sent his letters to William St. John his under sheriff [from whom Kemeys had been extorting money] requiring him thereby that the bailiffs of Cardiff and Llantrisant, being two of the servants of the said Nicholas Herbert, to return and impanel an inquest upon the said Llywelyn's death and accordingly sent to him a precept therein included, wherein was written the names of the Jurors, And that the said St. John should confer and be directed by the said Sr. Wm. Herbert and Mr. Nich. Herbert his cousins, that their friends might be at no disadvantage and to foresee that such should be jurors as were the friends of the said Sir. Wm. and Mr. Nich. Herbert.

The letter referred to was delivered by Sir William Herbert's servant to the under-sheriff at Nicholas Herbert's house in Sir William's presence. This is what the letter said:

> Cousin St. John — this evening about five of the Clock, I received a letter and precept which herein closed I send you, and in all your panels foresee to put so many of Sir William's friends that if any matter be offered none prevail against him. Among others be sure to return some of the twenty four here enclosed, but in any case be first directed by Sir William and my cousin Nicholas Herbert, that their friends be at no disadvantage. Extend your favour against the murderers, but in any case keep close this my direction.

Kemeys was to provide another packed jury later on, this time for the special petty sessions which were presided over by Sir William Herbert. But this time, Kemeys, like the Herberts, found that he had gone too far. Star Chamber dealt with him severely. 'The said Kemeys shall stand and be committed to the prison of the Fleet, as also pay five hundred pounds for a fine to Her Majesty.' Also 'he shall satisfy to the said Hawkins an hundred marks [£66 13s. 4d.] damages and . . . shall be removed out of the Commission of the peace until the right honourable the lord keeper shall be better satisfied of his behaviour'.

Edward Kemeys had been sheriff four times in Elizabeth's reign. There is proof that he packed juries for his friends and relatives. There is evidence that he sold offices and practised blackmail, though it must be stressed once again that to use Star Chamber documents, which often record only one side of the case, is bound to lead to exaggeration and distortion. It must also be noted that Kemeys is as bad an example of a dishonest sheriff as Elizabethan Wales can provide. But if the consistency and scope of his abuse are unique, the fact of corruption is not. There are signs that all sorts of local officials were prepared to abuse the law which they were theoretically upholding, particularly if their own interests were at stake. The story of Edward Kemeys reflects a society which still tended to settle disputes by force, and traditionally employed retainers whose conduct often sparked off trouble. It recalls a society in which wealth and influence, particularly when combined with official position, could mean evasion and often defiance of the law. Above all, it reveals a society in which standards of official conduct were not always high, in which inefficiency in local government was occasionally the despair of the central agencies. On the other hand, Kemeys paid the penalty for his misdeeds, and so did the Herberts. Furthermore, there is a suspicion that in cases of abuse of office court records survive in far greater quantity than, for example, family correspondence, which might give another side to the picture. These officials had a mass of official work to get through, for which they were unpaid and which was in addition to the management of their own estates and affairs. The officials who were hardest worked and on whom, in the last resort, the good government of Elizabethan Wales rested, were the J.P.s.

The office of J.P. was an old one but its introduction to Wales came only just before the act of Union. It was the act itself which gave statutory recognition to the office in all the Welsh counties, fixing the maximum number to be appointed in any one county at eight. This soon proved to be a totally inadequate quota to cope with the ever increasing load of work which the justices were expected to do; even so, the Welsh counties in Elizabeth's reign had few justices compared with English ones. In 1580 the smallest number of J.P.s in an English county was thirteen — in Rutland. In 1581 the average number for the Welsh counties was not much higher than this: Carmarthen had most with twenty-four; Cardigan least with nine. Flint had eighteen, Denbigh seventeen, Montgomery sixteen, Merioneth eleven, Caernarvon seventeen, Anglesey ten, Pembroke eleven, Glamorgan fourteen, Brecon fifteen and Radnor sixteen. There are probably two main reasons for the increase in number beyond the statutory eight. Firstly, there is no doubt that local gentry wanted to be J.P.s. There was status and influence in the office, even though the J.P. was hard worked and unpaid. In Glamorgan, for example, representatives of the important gentry families held office almost without a break during the sixteenth century; those in the list for Glamorgan in 1581 included Sir Edward Mansel, Sir Edward Stradling and Sir William Herbert. Herbert's son, Nicholas Herbert, was also a J.P., as was Anthony Mansel, Sir Edward's brother. The other justices of Glamorgan were all gentlemen, most of then substantial gentry such as William Mathew, Thomas Lewis, Edward Kemeys (whose exploits as sheriff have been described), Miles Button, William Carne, William Bassett, Lyson Price and Jenkin Franklin. It is true that it was not as easy in all Welsh counties to find such obvious gentry material to fill the commission of the peace, and certainly the general economic status of the Welsh J.P.s was inferior to that of those in English counties, but this, of course, only made the prize of office more attractive. The importance of the office is also illustrated by the keenness shown by those appointed as J.P. in using their power. Justices were appointed by the lord chancellor on the advice of the president and Council in the Marches and existing justices. Advice was readily available from these quarters and members of the Council in particular were very conscious of the fact that

J.P.s were sometimes appointed without their approval. Furthermore, as with the appointment of deputy-lieutenants and sheriffs, men of national standing who had influence in Wales tried to put their own men on the commission of the peace either as a reward for services rendered or in order to extend their power if the need arose. So, in Elizabeth's reign the earl of Essex built up a loyal faction of J.P.s in south-west Wales, four in Carmarthenshire and five in Cardiganshire. The earl of Leicester used his influence to obtain office for loyal supporters in north Wales. There can be no doubt, then, that the great magnates, the Council in the Marches and the justices themselves were very conscious of the importance and potential of the post.

The volume of work expected of the justices in Elizabeth's reign is the second reason for the growth in their number. Each of the hundreds in a county (there were ten in Glamorgan, for example) was the responsibility of three justices, each one, of course, serving more than one hundred. He had responsibility for a range of administrative and judicial duties in both the hundred and the county as a whole. He was helped only by the high constable and constables, who were appointed by the parishes to serve unpaid.

7   In his administrative capacity, a justice was on the receiving end of a constant stream of orders from such bodies as the Privy Council and the Council in the Marches, which relied largely on the J.P.s to put into effect any government decisions. According to the most famous Tudor authority on the office of J.P., William Lambarde, there were 306 statutes which had to be made effective by justices, including all the Poor Law legislation of Elizabeth's reign. In religious matters, J.P.s were responsible for fining non-attenders at church and reporting to the Privy Council on any relic or object of 'superstition' associated with Roman Catholicism. Working at least in pairs they were responsible for supervising the work of the sheriffs. The judicial duties of J.P.s were probably even more demanding. Put simply, these included enforcing the law of the land, investigating a wide range of offences, and hearing and judging breaches of the law either personally or in court.

J.P.s did a lot of their work by themselves or in small groups. They had very wide powers. A single J.P. could gaol suspects, issue warrants to sheriffs or bailiffs to arrest offenders, examine people about theft, excessive drinking or illegal hunting. Acting in pairs, they had wider responsibilities still. They could deal with such things as riots, evasions of subsidy payments (taxes levied by the monarch) and bail for prisoners.

The gentry of Wales played an active part in the court of quarter sessions. Records of these courts have generally disappeared, but those for the county of Caernarvonshire have survived and enable historians to generalise safely about how they worked. The role of the J.P. is crucial at this level since he was responsible for holding the sessions four times a year as laid down by the act of Union. Unlike great sessions, similar dates were not adhered to every year. Two or more justices decided on a suitable date for the meeting and then issued a writ to the sheriff. It was his duty to proclaim the date and place of the sessions and, through lesser officials such as constables, to ensure that all those required to attend did so.

The courts were held in the shire hall, and in theory most of the local officials of the county should have been there; in practice, as few as two or three J.P.s usually attended, along with the deputy-sheriff. A number of the gentry — or at least the better-off yeomen of the county — would also be there as jurors for the county. There were juries for each hundred as well. These were the juries of inquiry which decided the material to be put before the justices. The first cases the justices looked at involved prisoners brought from the gaol in the sheriff's custody who had stolen articles valued at less than 1s. Thefts involving more valuable goods were passed on to the great sessions.

Apart from the trial of prisoners, there would be a number of cases of assault or trespass, in which the accused person should have come to court to answer the charge. However, only a small number actually turned up, and as a result writs were issued session after session until eventually the accused appeared or was outlawed — the greatest penalty the justices could impose. There was also routine business such as licensing alehouses.

The court of quarter sessions took on a wider significance in Elizabeth's reign. Justices made more effort to attend and, once there, discussed matters of general importance to the county in addition to their judicial work. In court they heard all kinds of cases, including murder, assault, theft, witchcraft, vagrancy and failure to attend church. Punishments were harsh, varying from the stocks or flogging to hanging — even for petty thefts.

9

It is difficult to imagine just how dependent Elizabethan society was on the J.P. as an instrument of administration and justice in the absence of any kind of local, paid civil service or police force. Perhaps the best way of gaining an insight into how involved in government county gentlemen could be is to look at a sample of the letters they received. Family papers do not survive in any great quantity for Elizabeth's reign, but the Wynn and Clenennau papers and the Stradling Correspondence provide some evidence. Sir Edward Stradling's incoming letters give ample proof of the volume and variety of work involved.

The notabilities of central government made regular requests to Sir Edward. In 1574 Sir Henry Sidney, president of the Council in the Marches, asked Stradling to deal with criminals who had evaded capture and who had disregarded processes served on them by the Council. He was also asked to attend to military matters, involving the collection of armour and weapons, though this was rather in his capacity as sheriff of Glamorgan. The earl of Pembroke, who succeeded Sidney as lord president, made similar demands. In 1582, when there had been a riot involving a member of the Bassett family of Beaupré and five of the Bassetts of St. Athan, Stradling was one of two justices detailed to examine the case, 'being . . . in commission of the peace and near to all the parties.' In 1586, Walsingham asked Stradling to call before him two men who had not paid the fees of William Saunders, a servant in H.M. Chamber who had been detailed to bring these men before the justices in Somerset. The bishop of Llandaff in 1583 complimented Stradling on his capture of 'a very disobedient subject to her Highness'.

Both as J.P. and sheriff Stradling was frequently asked to

serve writs. Lord Buckhurst, subsequently lord treasurer of England, asked him to serve process on Anthony Morley for fraud in October 1583, 'understanding that you are Sheriff of Glamorganshire'. In 1576 Sir Oliver St. John of Bletsoe, who held lands in Penmark, Glamorgan, asked that Stradling help William Skydmore, the bearer of the letter, who had a good title to lands near Swansea, to get processes served on a rival claimant. Again, in 1583, Sir George Bromley of Worcestershire wrote to Stradling asking for process to be served on one of the Carnes on behalf of a Mistress Blunt.

Unfortunately, we have no way of knowing Stradling's response to these constant requests, but his patience must have been sorely tried by the earl of Worcester when the earl engaged his help in serving processes against Philip Bowen. On 25 February 1583 Worcester enclosed two processes in a letter, asking that they be served. On 16 April of the same year Worcester changed his mind, having had assurances from Bowen that the complaint would be met — probably involving the payment of a debt. On 31 May Worcester again asked that process be served, since Bowen's promises had come to nothing. By 28 August Worcester had once more decided not to serve the processes owing to 'special suit made for him [Bowen]', and he asked for their return. Stradling's reactions can be imagined when, in October 1583, Philip Bowen himself delivered a letter to Stradling from Worcester asking that the dues which were payable to Worcester as lord marcher should be paid to Bowen, who had the earl of Worcester's warrant.

There are records of mistakes being made and subsequently being put right. Stradling had taken possession of some brazil wood at the request of Sir William and Nicholas Herbert. They subsequently found that the wood had been lawfully acquired and asked for it to be returned. William and John Webbar were brought before Stradling after being captured by hue and cry for having stolen a mare in Devon. They were found to be innocent. The variety of jobs is particularly noticeable. There was judgement to be passed in the case of a cow stolen from Cefn Mabli; a ship to be prevented from leaving Swansea docks; evidence to be given at assizes; disputes over the ownership of cattle to be settled.

There is ample evidence in Stradling's letters of the extent of the lawlessness and disorder that so often produced despair from the authorities, and Stradling and his fellow justices were constantly involved in trying to do something about the situation. Two letters, one from Edmund Walter, a chief justice of great sessions, and one from Sir Thomas Mansel are particularly illuminating. Walter asked for an interview with Stradling before the great sessions met in Cardiff in order to decide what procedure should be adopted at the sessions for the punishment of offenders in Glamorgan, 'considering the late disorders and garboyles committed within that county'. Sir Thomas Mansel's problem was that he had been called away to London on urgent business and was anxious that no disorder should occur while he was away. Therefore, he asked Stradling to look after his tenants so that 'the rich shall not oppress the poor, and that the poor injure not the wealthy', a revealing comment on responsibility in contemporary Glamorgan society.

As a result of a combination of official position and personal influence, Stradling wielded considerable local power, though here again national influence intruded. In July 1578, Dr. David Lewis, judge of the Admiralty and principal of Jesus College, Oxford, asked Stradling for his assent to the appointment of David Morgan as gaoler in Glamorgan. But complications soon arose out of this simple request. For some reason, disputes occurred over a period of years involving the gaolership and Stradling figured prominently in them. David Morgan owed his influence to the fact that he was related to Blanche Parry, one of Queen Elizabeth's favourite gentlewomen. And Blanche was related to Stradling. In April 1579, the queen had granted the gaolership to Morgan for life and all seemed well. Blanche Parry seemed well satisfied when she wrote to Stradling asking that he continue his favour towards Morgan. Four years elapsed before the next development. In January 1583, Sir Valentine Dale, master of the court of Requests, informed Stradling that he had heard there was a dispute between Stradling and Morgan over the gaolership of the county. The problem appeared to be that in 1583 Stradling was sheriff of Glamorgan and, as sheriff, had to work very closely with the gaoler. Dale tried to impress on him that this situation could only last for a year, since that was Stradling's term of office, and therefore he should be patient and co-operate with his subordinate. Dale strongly advised him not to dismiss Morgan because the queen had given him his office as a special favour. Dale followed up with another letter four days later, which was also signed by Judge David Lewis. Morgan had complained to the court of Requests that Stradling would not allow him to do the job which the queen had granted him, nor receive the fees which went with it. Stradling should come to London to answer these charges but Dale and Lewis spared him this because of his responsibilities as sheriff. Nevertheless, they strongly advised Stradling to allow Morgan to continue in office or 'show us sufficient cause in law of your refusal'.

Stradling's letters provide an insight into many aspects of the [10] work of a gentleman who enjoyed official position in local government and the administration of justice throughout Elizabeth's reign. There is evidence of a great deal of hard, varied work, and of some less official methods of dealing with local problems such as personal contact between the gentry themselves and the notabilities of central government at Ludlow and Westminster. There is evidence of the local influence wielded by [11] the gentry and often, too, of the touchiness and pride which could turn even the more law-abiding of them into lawbreakers. The machinery of good government existed in Elizabethan Wales and, in theory, the administration of government and justice in the country was well looked after by a hierarchy of central institutions and local officials. But it is clear that there was a considerable gap between theory and practice. There is no doubt that the system worked — often smoothly, relatively quickly and always without complete breakdown. This in itself was a remarkable achievement and an indication of how far the interests of the gentry and of the state coincided. On the other hand, a general identity of interest was a very different thing from continuous co-operation and devotion to duty. The gentry had too many other responsibilities.

Chapter V

Gentry Attitudes: Defence, Piracy, Religion

Elizabethan Wales, as we have seen, had no paid bureacracy or police force. Government by volunteer was bound to produce tensions between public responsibility and private interest. In three key areas of government it is possible to identify different aspects of this tension, aspects which are essential to an understanding of the gentry's role in government.

Everyone involved in national or local government accepted that defence of the realm was a matter of priority; but local officials had other pressing responsibilities. In particular, they had to attend to the running of their estates which provided them with their livelihood. The result was that, without malicious intent, they were often dilatory in implementing orders of the central government and the Council in the Marches relating to defence. The problem of piracy was in a different category. To some unscrupulous Welsh gentlemen it offered opportunity for personal profit even though their public responsibility was to capture pirates. Indeed, the rights which went with office could be used to shield pirates. The religious tensions of Elizabeth's reign are well known and the national problem was reflected at local level. Many of the Welsh gentry kept their Catholic sympathies yet were responsible for enforcing anti-Catholic legislation. Bearing in mind the presence of such attitudes among the gentry, we can now look at each problem in more detail.

12   Defence was a pressing problem in Elizabethan Wales. We have already seen how this subject figures prominently on the agenda of the Council in the Marches. There were many

reasons for this. In the first place, there was a pretty constant threat of invasion throughout Elizabeth's reign and the authorities at Ludlow and in London were almost entirely dependent on local officials. The only way in which the Council in the Marches could keep abreast of military developments in the counties was by prompt reports from county gentlemen. These often did not appear or, if they did, were often so incomplete that they were of little value and led to requests for further reports. Secondly, the state and distribution of armour in the counties left much to be desired. The expense involved in buying armour was sufficient to deter the local gentry from keeping up the county stocks and it was often impossible at times of musters, when the armour was inspected, to produce the necessary quantity. Thirdly, there was the constant problem of the fitness of soldiers, particularly those who went on foreign service to Ireland or the Netherlands. The able-bodied men in the counties between the ages of sixteen and sixty formed a militia, a small section of which comprised the 'trained Bands', which had special training and were the core of county defence. These aspects of military duty were tolerably acceptable to the inhabitants, even though the militia system was unconstitutional; but problems arose when men from the militia had to be chosen for foreign service. Not only did this mean social disruption or loss of livelihood — with crops not planted and harvest neglected — but conditions in the army were such that men would do almost anything to avoid being recruited. This was even before they took into account the possibility of death or, even worse in the sixteenth century, serious injury. There is no mistaking the agitation which this attitude caused among commanders as well as among soldiers. When Sir William Morgan, of Penycoed in Monmouthshire, was appointed to lead an army to Ireland in 1579, he was very apprehensive about the quality of the men from south Wales who would be serving under him and the state of their equipment. He was par- ticularly concerned lest their armour, powder and shot be inadequate, and even that they might be so badly clothed and short of money that 'they may perish for want'. Fourthly, people liable to be recruited for service abroad were prepared to take any possible measures to avoid it and this is where the pressure sometimes proved too great for the gentry. Sir John Perrot of Carew, who was constantly feuding with his fellows and who could be particularly unscrupulous, was an offender in this matter as in so much else. When he left for Ireland in 1570 he forced as many as possible of his enemies' servants to go with him. In Brian Howells' words, 'all those reviewed at the musters were asked whether they were or had ever been against him: if they answered in the negative they were released with a caution that they were to remain in that state'.

A further notorious case was before Star Chamber in the first year of Elizabeth's reign. It belongs to a period before the regular appointment of deputy-lieutenants, when raising men depended heavily on recruiting the retainers of gentry families. The story begins with William Herbert, earl of Pembroke, who brought the Herbert family to a position of power at Court, in Wiltshire and in Glamorgan. The case came to Star Chamber because Sir Thomas Stradling of St. Donat's took up a plea on behalf of some of his tenants, and there is no doubt that family rivalry had as much to do with his action as any concern for the law. The evidence is slanted in favour of the complainant. Nevertheless, some of it is striking. It appears that the earl of Pembroke, after having been appointed to command an expedition to France in 1557, asked for a muster of his own men in Glamorgan to be carried out by his close relative, William Herbert of Cogan Pill. Stradling's complaint was that all kinds of illegal activities had gone on under the guise of this muster. It should, of course, have been confined to the earl's tenants in Glamorgan, but Stradling alleged that Herbert had given orders to constables to raise a sum of £1,000 indiscriminately. The ostensible purpose of this large sum was to provide 100 footmen with equipment. Stradling went on to claim that those refusing to pay had their goods and possessions confiscated and, further, that Herbert made a considerable profit by accepting bribes from those men who wanted to be left out of the muster. Neither women nor orphans were spared from the money contribution and, said Stradling, there was great impoverishment as a result. Five of his men who had been affected by the muster took out actions of trespass against the constable concerned for wrongful seizure of their possessions. They had no success because, they maintained, 'the said William Herbert is nephew to my Lord of Pembroke', and hence, they 'could have nobody in that county that would be Attorney in Court for them, nor of Counsel with them therein, lest my said Lord should be offended with them in so doing'.

There were other accusations. It was alleged that four noteable gentry of Glamorgan, William Herbert, Sir George Herbert, Edward Lewis and James Button, who had been requested by Pembroke to provide men for military service in France, called before them the gentlemen of the hundreds of Neath, Newcastle, Ogmore, Cowbridge, Dinas Powys, Llantrisant and Cardiff, and told them that the earl of Pembroke needed 500 men, some of them armed, and that the expense would be borne by the inhabitants.

In response to these complaints, the court of Star Chamber acted in the normal way by appointing three investigators, all men of some standing in the county: John Carne, Roger Williams and William Bassett. They did a sterling job, taking evidence from all the areas affected in the county. Their first problem was to get an accurate account of the money which had been collected by Pembroke's men, but these latter either refused to give the information or stated that they had lost their accounts. The main part of the investigation, however, centred on the evidence taken from witnesses, and some of their statements are very revealing, even when we accept the need to treat Star Chamber depositions carefully. Robert Gamage of Coity said that he had been told to appear at Cardiff and was there informed that the earl of Pembroke needed 500 men, some to be equipped with corselets (body armour) which would cost £3 6s. 8d. for each man. He was then asked how much he could pay towards the cost. His offer was to the value of eight silver rivets, but the commissioners demanded the price of ten corselets. When he refused, the commissioners threatened to raise the money themselves on his possessions and land. Gamage finally settled for forty marks (£26 13s. 4d.); he also paid £10 for his wife and father.

David Thomas Dee, high constable of Llangynwyd in Glamorgan, was forced by the commissioners to collect some of the money, and in the process was alleged to have caused a great deal of hardship and distress. When Lewis Deio refused to pay his dues, Dee took away eight sheep from his land and struck him with his sword. The people of Kenfig who refused to pay were hauled before the commissioners in Cardiff and forced to change their mind. David ap Jenkin of Llangatwg reported that one high constable took away the possessions of a poor woman; her husband was already away on service but this had made no difference. Such allegations were repeated time and time again by those interviewed by the commissioners.

It must be reiterated that historians who are familiar with Star Chamber proceedings constantly warn us of the problem of interpreting them. In this case, as in so many others, there is no record of the verdict. Naturally, it was in the interest of the person complaining to the court to put his case in the strongest possible terms. More than this: we know that even the London courts were used by gentry families to pursue their own private feuds and there was often very little love lost between the Stradlings and the Herberts. There can be no certainty that Herbert was guilty of the alleged crimes. There are, even so, some features of the case which are consistent with evidence from other contemporary sources. The earl of Pembroke's influence in Glamorgan was considerable, and his relatives were not slow to use this influence as a shield against the law. Military service was something to be feared and, if possible, avoided. In the situation bribes were offered and accepted. Money and influence could buy exemption. But this case and others like it reveal more than bribery at work. The rules of justice could sometimes be ignored by men such as Sir William Herbert when self-interest proved more attractive than public duty. Nevertheless, machinery existed for bringing even these families to justice and this was by no means the only occasion on which the Herberts encountered the court of Star Chamber to their cost.

Piracy was an activity which was widespread around the

coasts of Wales and there was a lot of money to be made from it. Something of its flavour can be gained by looking at the career of Captain Hugh Griffith. He was the third son of the squire of Cefnamlwch in Anglesey and had a remarkable career. His father apprenticed him to a merchant adventurer in London, and in due course he became a successful agent for several merchants in various parts of Europe. However, on one journey from London to the continent, he was imprisoned at Dunkirk and the large sum of £1,200 was taken from him. He was eventually released through the influence of another Welshman, Hugh Owen, but because he had been forced to pay a ransom, and therefore lost his money and his credit, he could not return to his career as a merchant. So, he managed to get a licence to fight Spanish ships on the high seas and capture any goods they might have on board. His death came after one of his battles with the Spaniards. He waylaid a ship taking treasure from Italy to Spain and, according to Sir John Wynn of Gwydir, the Elizabethan writer, after a battle of four or five days he cap- tured the ship, but at the cost of losing a number of his crew and being himself badly wounded. He had to take refuge in Algiers, where he died either (says Wynn suspiciously) 'of his hurts or was poisoned'. Wynn also records that one of Captain Griffith's followers returned home and told Wynn that he had been tortured and beaten with a 'bull's pessell' to make him confess. It was an eventful career.

The Spaniards would have regarded his activities as piracy on the high seas, but as far as the English government was con- cerned, Griffith had the queen's warrant to attack the Spanish. However, research on piracy in Wales in this period has shown that Griffith did not always stick to molesting Spanish ships and that he was not too concerned about how he disposed of captured goods.

As we have noted, Captain Hugh Griffith's father, Griffith John Griffith, was the head of the gentry family of Cefn- amlwch. It is almost certain that he was involved with his son in organised piracy. In 1599 Captain Griffith arrived off the north Wales coast in command of a ship with a crew of fifty, a stock of canvas and a mysterious 'treasure chest' on board. There was one small problem. The ship was a captured French vessel, not Spanish at all. Its capture had been an act of piracy. It was because of this that the Admiralty took a close interest in the festivities on board ship involving Hugh Griffith's father and several other close relatives, and in the presents they were given. Many of the relatives were promptly interviewed. One of them alleged that Captain Griffith's father had in fact financed the voyage. The witness then said that the day after Griffith sailed to Beaumaris, a naval vessel sailed into St. Tudwal's to look for him. John Griffith, Hugh's brother, rode to Beaumaris that night to warn him and he abandoned the ship and the crew dispersed. The evidence of John Griffith himself is, as one would expect, rather different. He argued that he believed the ship to be Spanish and that his visit to Beaumaris was pure coincidence, though he admitted telling his brother that a Captain Morgan had been looking for him. John Griffith's evidence also revealed that, while in Anglesey, Hugh Griffith had been a frequent guest at Sir Richard Bulkeley's house. It is typically tantalising that the story should end there. We know no more of Captain Hugh Griffith except Sir John Wynn's story of his dramatic death, very far from north Wales.

This episode, taken in conjunction with much other evidence, indicates just how the gentry could condone piracy and profit from it, even conspiring to ensure that pirates were not caught—indeed, financing their enterprises. As J.P.s and commissioners for piracy, their public duty was to try to capture pirates and their associates, but self-interest and family loyalty were often too strong to allow them to do so. A similar pattern is evident in other places. In the south-west Sir John Perrott, one of the most influential gentlemen of the area, made a considerable amount of money from the sale of pirated goods. In Glamorgan the earl of Pembroke's protection for some of his family enabled the gentry in Cardiff to profit from and protect John Callice, the famous Elizabethan pirate who operated mainly around the coasts of Wales. On the other hand, some local officials, like the Stradlings in Glamorgan, were zealous pirate-hunters. All in all, the Privy Council found it particularly difficult to control the activities of pirates round the

Welsh coast. The problems were enormous. There were any number of inlets and bays where pirated goods could be brought ashore from small ships of probably less than forty tons which regularly crossed the English Channel. There was the marginal distinction between capture of a French vessel, which could be piracy, and capture of a Spanish ship, which could be classed as legitimate action against an enemy. But above all, there was the part played by the gentry. The Cardiff commissioners for piracy in the mid-sixteenth century found it virtually impossible to get any of the inhabitants to talk. Too many important families profited, and it is more surprising, perhaps, that pirates of John Callice's fame were eventually caught than that they remained free for so many years. Even when Callice was eventually arrested he managed to persuade the government not to hang him.

The gentry were responsible for enforcing the religious laws as deputy-lieutenants and justices. Their duties included administering fines for non-attendance at church, keeping a close watch for foreign priests who might come to bolster up the Roman faith and generally making sure that recusants were watched, tried, fined or imprisoned. This responsibility posed problems for many gentlemen, problems of which the government itself was fully aware and which Queen Elizabeth herself appreciated.

The divided religious loyalties of the gentry were evident in both their private and their public lives. Many had strong Catholic sympathies — the Stradlings and many others in Glamorgan, the gentlemen of the Llŷn peninsula in north Wales, a number of the better known Cardiganshire and Pembrokeshire families, and branches of the Morgan family in Monmouthshire. But many of the most staunch Roman Catholic families were compromised to some extent in the early stages of the Reformation when they bought monastic lands. This was not such an obvious endorsement of the Reformation as, at first sight, it might appear because many gentlemen had already leased large areas of monastic land before the Reformation; but in the final analysis, it probably gave some of them a vested interest in the break with Rome.

The public compromise of the gentry lay in their acceptance of local office. This was an indication of the strength of family pride, and indeed of their self-interest. Just as the dissolution of the monasteries offered them a unique opportunity to improve their economic status, so the increased opportunities for office holding which the act of Union brought, held out the possibility of greater local influence and prestige. But at the same time there can be no doubt that the gentry felt a loyalty to the Crown and to the kind of government the Tudors brought to Wales. Nevertheless, it remains true that the acceptance of office involved — or should have involved — not only the acceptance of legislation which it suited the gentry to enforce, but also the acceptance of the whole of Tudor policy, political, economic and religious.

The tensions brought about by the clash between public and private interest were well enough understood by the queen and moderation in religious matters was one of the hallmarks of her policy. Her religious settlement was a compromise, and at different periods in her reign one sees Elizabeth taking a much less firm line on religious legislation than the Commons would have wished. There is no question that Elizabeth herself wanted some outward indication of compromise from her subjects, such as attendance at church; but she did not want to drive them too far by compelling attendance at communion.

[14]   This attitude provided something of an escape valve for many gentry families. Nevertheless, as Elizabeth's reign wore on, the religious situation deteriorated, particularly after 1570. Threats to the queen's life, the threat from Spain and from the increased activity of Roman Catholic priests in the country, meant that legislation became more severe and enforcement more important. In 1581 it became high treason to convert anyone from the Anglican to the Roman church. Absence from church carried with it a fine of £20 per month. To say mass, or to listen to it, could mean a year's imprisonment and a large fine on conviction. Later, any Catholic priest entering Britain was committing treason. In 1593 all recusants had to keep within

five miles of their home unless granted a special dispensation. It was the gentry of the counties who were responsible for putting this legislation into effect. But, at the same time, we have to remember the common opinion among historians of England and Wales that recusancy was only really a threat when there existed leadership — or at least approval — from local gentlemen. Only Monmouthshire of the Welsh counties caused the government anything like as much trouble as Lancashire or Cheshire, but none of them escaped the problem either.

The attitude of those gentry families with Catholic sympathies was by no means the only element in the story of religion in Elizabethan Wales; but there is no doubt that the queen's government was fully aware of its vulnerability when those involved in local administration were sometimes noted recusants. Reactions to Elizabeth's religious policy varied. The Welsh border counties and Flintshire had a recusant problem. In Caernarvonshire the gentry of the south, particularly in the Llŷn peninsula, had strong Catholic sympathies. They were friendly with, and gave support to, priests who came to north Wales and did much to keep Catholicism alive there. In the years following 1577, the Privy Council set out to tackle the Catholic problem in Caernarvonshire. The turning-point for the county gentry seems to have come after Thomas Owen of Plas Du, who kept virtual open house for seminary priests, was accused and tried. After this experience recusancy declined and, as it did so, the gentry concerned played an ever increasing part in local government.

In the diocese of Llandaff there were recusants among the influential gentry of Glamorgan and Monmouthshire. Sir Thomas Stradling's unorthodox religious activities have already been outlined. But one estimate claims that half the justices in the two counties were indifferent to the Church of England. There is no doubting the Catholic sympathies of many justices and sheriffs; Edward Lewis and Anthony Mansel are two examples. Others included Thomas Carne, frequently a J.P., three times sheriff of Glamorgan and twice M.P., who was convicted of recusancy. Four J.P.s, Thomas Lewis of the Van, Rowland Morgan of Machen, Edward Morgan of Llantarnam and Edward Kemeys of Cefn Mabli, were mentioned in 1585 as being recusants. Another indication of Romish sympathies among the gentry is the fact that most young men who went abroad to be trained as priests came from good families, one outstanding example being David Stradling of St. Donat's.

Despite the active co-operation of some gentry families in helping to keep the Catholic faith alive, it became apparent as Elizabeth's reign progressed that this was not to be a crucial factor in the government of Wales. There were enough deputy-lieutenants and justices who were prepared to enforce the law and bring recusants to trial. There was an increasing degree of compromise by the gentry themselves as a new generation came into public life. Fundamentally, it seems that the gentry were too involved with the ideals and aspirations of the Elizabethan state, their hopes too closely tied to Elizabethan policy, for their religion to drive them into open defiance on a scale which threatened the state. As Glanmor Williams writes, 'Only a successful campaign amongst the gentry could have turned the tide in favour of the old faith. But they showed no enthusiasm for opening their doors to the seminary priests or their doctrines. And they had good reason for their reluctance.'

The fact that recusancy did not pose a real threat to the stability of Elizabethan Wales does not mean that the gentry eagerly endorsed the religious settlement. Protestant enthusiasts levelled various accusations against them. Bishop Richard Davies's report of 1570 might serve to sum up the complaints. Produced for the Privy Council, which was anxiously assessing religious affiliations in the wake of the rising of the Northern Earls, this report revealed that in the diocese of St. David's at least central government had little to fear. Davies reported that none of the major families refused to attend church but many were indifferent to the fortunes of Protestantism. He castigated local officials, particularly sheriffs and J.P.s, for doing little to stamp out papistry, idolatry and pilgrimages. Furthermore, lay impropriation and the poverty of livings, taken together with the lack of religious literature in Welsh, militated against the spread of Protestant teachings. These were problems for which the gentry bore some responsibility. When they had leased or bought monastic land they took over the tithes of those parishes which had been appropriated by the monasteries in the middle ages. They were therefore responsible for appointing and paying the clergymen who served those parishes. The temptation was to leave the living vacant or to pay the incumbent badly. Poor pay meant a lack of well-educated clergy, who were able to exist only by holding a number of livings; therefore they could serve no single parish satisfactorily. It must be remembered, however, that the gentry were responsible for filling only a minority of livings and that they were not responsible for the fundamental poverty which afflicted all the Welsh dioceses.

Protestantism could only succeed in Wales if there was an adequate religious literature in Welsh; and it had to be available not in the rare manuscripts of the middle ages but in the plentiful supply made possible by the printing press. Sir John Price, a prosperous gentleman who had acquired most of the lands of Brecon Priory at the dissolution, had pointed the way in the first half of the sixteenth century. He was attracted by Protestantism and was determined that the printing press should be used to bring at least some religious literature, such as the creed and the ten commandments, to the Welsh people. Price's contribution was *Yn y llyfr hwn,* the first book to be published in Welsh. His example was followed in Elizabeth's reign by other laymen, the greatest of whom was William Salesbury. Salesbury's production of moral and spiritual writings in Welsh culminated in his major contribution to the Welsh New Testament, which appeared in 1567. He it was, too, who argued that the ancient Britons had possessed the scriptures in Welsh, a claim which was a first step towards Bishop Richard Davies's theory that the Protestant church was the pure, uncorrupted church of ancient Britain, established within thirty years of Christ's death.

The contribution of laymen to the provision of religious literature in Elizabethan Wales was remarkable; and many gentry realised the importance of such literature. B. G. Charles says of George Owen that 'He was a staunch Protestant . . . and yet not punctilious in the observance of Church doctrine and certainly no Puritan . . .'. He then quotes Owen's reaction to the translation of the Bible into Welsh:

> Now not three years past we have the light of the gospel, yea the whole Bible, in our native tongue which in short time must needs work great good inwardly in the hearts of the people, whereas the service and sacraments in the English tongue were as strange to many or most of the simplest sort as the mass in the time of blindness was to the rest of England.

George Owen's religious attitudes were not untypical of Welshmen of his class. In Glanmor Williams's words,

> . . . the key to the gentry's role lies not in religion but in government. They could not separate the question of authority in the Church from that of authority in the state and in society . . . What really counted with most of the Welsh gentry was the security of the political and social order from threats internal and external. Its stability was guaranteed in their eyes by the successful liaison between their pre-eminence in the locality and royal jurisdiction at the centre . . . That alignment was not imperilled by anything in the Reformation changes of the Tudor state.

Conclusion

That there was a successful liaison between those responsible for central and local government in Wales cannot be in doubt. The breakdown in that liaison did not come in Elizabeth's reign. Nevertheless, two questions will always provoke argument among historians. Firstly, was the co-operation of the gentry with the Elizabethan state bought at too high a price? Religious conformity, part of that price, was discussed in the last chapter; but the language issue is far more contentious. Secondly, how successful was the partnership? While there was never complete breakdown, there were occasions when parts of Wales were perilously close to anarchy. There is no final answer to either question; but there are salient factors which must be borne in mind when they are discussed.

The most emotive issue associated today with changes in sixteenth-century Welsh government is that of the Welsh language. The language of government in Elizabeth's reign was officially English. The records of the central courts, the Council in the Marches, the courts of great sessions and quarter sessions were kept in English and, less frequently, Latin. Gentry correspondence relating to matters of government was in English. The language clause of the act of Union was being observed to this extent.

Gentry involvement in government meant that they grew more anglicised as their contacts with London and, in greater number, with Ludlow increased. More gentlemen were anxious to master English; there was considerable incentive to do so. However, there were other anglicising influences at work which were only marginally associated with government. The most important of these was education. The gentry frequented grammar schools, universities and the inns of court in ever-increasing numbers in the sixteenth century. There is some evidence that they favoured English schools at the expense of Welsh ones. There is dispute as to why so many gentlemen frequented the universities and inns of court in Elizabeth's reign; probably it was because of a complex mixture of realism and idealism. Some doubtless believed that a university education would enable them to participate more competently in local government. Some were influenced by that Renaissance humanism which was idealised in Castiglione's *The Courtier* — the educated polymath involved, as duty decreed, in the government of his state. Some probably went because it was 'the done thing'. Again, there were genuine scholars among the gentry. There is further dispute as to the profit they derived from this element in their education. It has been argued that for the majority of gentlemen the length of their stay at university or inn was too short and their attitude too frivolous to equip them to carry out their responsibilities in administration and government. This is almost certainly over-stating the case, but one thing is certain: the only universities were Oxford and Cambridge and they had an anglicising influence.

Whatever the historian's verdict on the language issue, he must take into account what is known of the attitude of the gentry themselves. They do not seem to have been aware of any problem. Sir John Price of Brecon, writing a little before Elizabeth's reign, apparently saw no incongruity in being involved in the government of England and Wales at the highest level and being vitally concerned with the provision of religious literature in Welsh. To Price, the language was of secondary importance; it was merely the vehicle for bringing the scriptures to the Welsh people. The crucial factor was the nation's religious need. This corresponds with William Salesbury's attitude to the Welsh language. He regarded the provision of a Welsh Bible as indispensable to the progress of Protestantism. He saw a crisis confronting the Welsh language; but he did not see it in terms of whether Welsh could survive as the language of the people, the language of everyday speech. To this outstanding Renaissance scholar the crisis was whether Welsh could be so adapted as to become the language of humanism and the new learning in Wales. That English was the language of government was not a cause for concern. It is important to remember that writers like George Owen, Sir John Wynn and Sir Edward Stradling who wrote in English were also beneficent patrons of Welsh poets: Stradling financed the publication of a Welsh grammar. No one would deny that the process of anglicisation among the gentry was accelerated during the sixteenth century; but, by the end of Elizabeth's reign, it did not mean that they were severed from their roots in Welsh society.

Finally, how successful was Elizabethan government in Wales? Here again the issue is contentious, but one thing is certain. The attitudes of the county gentry to the law were crucial; Elizabethan government and the enforcement of justice depended on these gentlemen. As we have seen, there was a hierarchy of authority with a number of checks and balances, but a crucial role was played by the county officials. On the credit side, it has to be remembered that, in general, they co-operated voluntarily with the central authority at least to the extent that there was no irrevocable breakdown. The gentry were not paid officials; indeed, an office such as that of sheriff could prove quite an expensive burden to the holder. In any society it is the corrupt official who tends to become im-mortalised in the records, the heretic whose beliefs are re-membered, the pirate who has a halo of glamour. It was the gentry of Wales who ensured that there was never anarchy in the country, though defiance of the Council in the Marches sometimes lasted for months. It is true that there is no means of knowing what might have happened if the military resources of the Welsh counties had been put to the test by an invasion. But we do know that on the whole the gentry's interests were suf-ficiently in tune with those of the government for recusants to be brought to trial, for justice to be meted out regularly and often impartially, particularly to the less influential members of society. We know that men, often admittedly of dubious quality, were trained for, and sent on, military service, that the poor law was administered, that members were elected to parliament; in short, that the Welsh justices, sheriffs and deputy-lieutenants got through a considerable amount of time-consuming, taxing and complex work.

The fact that such work was unpaid is especially significant because of the considerable economic pressures which gentlemen were under in the Elizabethan period. Their resources, the size of their estates and the fertility of their land varied enormously, of course, and local officials could be drawn from the ranks of impoverished gentry from the Llŷn peninsula as well as well-to-do families from the vale of Glamorgan. Nevertheless, they all had to face a difficult economic situation. The steep rise in prices meant that the majority of gentry, whose agricultural and financial resources gave them no cushion against inflation, had to be careful managers of their estates. They had to keep a close watch on their tenants' rents and, whenever possible, increase them to match rising prices. They had to ensure that their tenants farmed efficiently and that the land they themselves farmed was made to produce the maximum return. The prudent gentleman kept a close eye on his family budget so that any tendency towards extravagance was curbed. In short, in small estates and large, the economic conditions of Elizabeth's reign were such that the gentry could prosper if they were prepared to put time and effort into the running of their estates. This was their first responsibility. It is hardly surprising, therefore, that the duties of local government should sometimes take second place or be postponed or tackled grudgingly and inadequately. The likelihood of this happening when unpopular responsibilities were involved — such as mustering men — was that much greater.

There is another side to these economic pressures. Land was precious. It was worth fighting over and disputes over title to land were common. Courts like the court of Exchequer existed to deal with rival claims, but we know from the records of these courts that the gentry often used force to press their claims. Again, this must be set against the background of a society whose methods of settling disputes were often outside the law. Bullying, exploitation, violence and bribery were time-honoured features of life in Wales and the elaborate Tudor system of enforcing the law could not eradicate lawlessness. Because gentlemen were more prominent, because many of them still kept small bands of retainers, because they had more opportunity as officers to use the law for their own ends, they have left considerable evidence of how they betrayed their trust. But often that evidence is culled from the records of courts like Star Chamber, and provides proof that even the most influential of families could be brought to justice. The most obvious flaw in the system was not so much that the gentry abused their responsibilities, but that after being found out and punished, they were able to make a come-back and enter the commission of the peace and the shrievalty. Ally to this the influence of faction and family rivalries, and the key to much of the bad government of the period is found.

There can be no clear-cut answer to the question of how well the gentry ran Wales in the second half of the sixteenth century. The situation changed from decade to decade and from county to county, depending on accidents of death or geography or family connection. There are many indications of inefficiency, of blatant disregard for the due processes of law. Nevertheless, there is much evidence of a responsible attitude to local administration. It emerges in the records of the courts of great sessions and quarter sessions. It springs from the few family papers which survive. In a period of considerable upheaval, economic, religious and political, both the machinery and personnel of the system of government and justice outlined in the act of Union were adequate to meet the remarkably diverse demands made on them in Elizabethan Wales.

Illustrative Documents

[1] *A Forthcoming Merionethshire Election, 1571.*

At Ludlow, 14 March 1571.

Whereas the Council is informed that there is great labour and suit in Merionethshire concerning the next election of Knights of the shire for Parliament, and danger that by outward signs and tokens of brag a proper election will be prevented. The Council had thought wise to commission certain people to be present and take note of every one who should infringe the laws against rioting and carrying arms in assemblies and thereupon to report to the Council. But on consideration of the authority and charge of the Sheriff and Justices of the Peace, the not doing of their duties not being had in suspicion before some trial thereof, it is decided to trust to them. Therefore letters are to be sent out rehearsing this and commanding the Sheriff to make proclamation at the time of the election against any breach of the peace and especially against the carrying of weapons on pain of penalties provided by statute. If any disturbance should arise the Sheriff and Justices are to use correction therein as the law has appointed and after being thus warned they will be held responsible for any disorder.

From R. Flenley (ed.), *A Calendar of the Register of the Queen's Majesty's Council in the Dominion and Principality of Wales and the Marches of the Same* (London, 1916), pp. 94-95.

[2] *The Privy Council stresses the need for vigilance on the part of J.P.s, 1571.*

In consequence of the benefit from the diligent execution last year of the laws against vagabonds and sturdy beggars and the disorders of the last winter resultant on less strict carrying out of these laws, you, [the Council in the Marches] with the Justices of the Peace, are again ordered to be more diligent within the next three months of August, September and October. On the 20th August, strict watch is to be kept, as well throughout the shire as in places exempt, from 7 p.m. to 3 o'clock next afternoon by Constables and two, three or more of the most substantial parishioners. All rogues, vagabonds and masterless men are to be arrested and punished by stocking and sharp and severe whipping according to the laws, afterwards sending them on, from Constable to Constable, until they reach their native place or last abode within three years according to the statute. Similarly action shall be taken on the 12th September and October and then each 15 or 20 days, not omitting to punish any vagabond found between the specified times. From time to time you shall notify the Privy Council of your action in the matter, not failing in the execution of the goodly and zealous pleasure of the Queen as you shall answer for it. Hampton Court, 30th July 1571. Your loving friends T. Sussex, R. Leicester, F. Clynton, W. Howarde, W. Burghley, F. Knoles, T. Smyth.

From Flenley, p. 96.

3 *The Council in the Marches as a court of law, 1594.*

This Council, although it bear the name of Council, is not so much occupied in matters of Council, as it is in hearing and determining of matters of right. For it is now used and grown to be an ordinary Court of Justice for every man to sue in; and is much like in authority to the Court called the Chancery in Westminster, which is a court of equity to mitigate the vigour of Law in divers causes. The authority and jurisdiction of this Council is not certainly known: for they are to judge and determine of such matters as the Queen of England shall authorise them from time to time by way of instructions, and their authority is not certain. But most commonly they deal for all manner of misdemeanours, as assaults and affrays, riots, routs, forcible entries, briberies, extortions, comorthas, exactions, and all manner of outrages and misdemeanours committed within their commission. And therein they resemble much in authority the high and noble Court of Star Chamber at Westminster. They also deal in mitigating, as I said before, of all extremities and rigorousness of the Common Law of this land, as extreme dealings upon penal bonds and such like. It also determineth detaining of evidences where there is no remedy at the common law. It examineth the title of lands, depending upon the same; it taketh order for the speedy trial and pleading of matters at the common law: also it holdeth plea for debt without specialty, detaining of goods or chattels: it forceth evil dealing tutors to yield account to fatherless infants of their goods and debt: it examineth witnesses to remain of record *ad perpetuam rei memoriam;* and which is most beneficial of all other matters, it taketh speedy remedy for restoring or stalling of possessions of lands or tenements, which otherwise would be long ere they might recover their lawful possessions by ordinary course at the common law. It also punisheth the vices of incest, adultery and fornication. And generally it is the very place of refuge for the poor oppressed of this country of Wales to fly unto. And for this cause it is as greatly frequented with suits as any one Court at Westminster whatsoever the more for that it is the best cheap court in England for fees: and there is great speed made in trial of all causes. For they divide their sittings for matters in hearing into four terms, agreeable to those for England in number, though not agreeable in time . . .

This court is it which at the beginning brought Wales to that civility and quietness that you now see it, from that wild and outrageous state that you shall read of. And although some think it an unnecessary court at this present, considering the obedience that Wales is now brought unto, and fitter to be dissolved than continued, doubtless they are far mistaken therein, unless there were some other courts of like authority erected for punishment of divers the offences aforesaid . . . .

From George Owen, *The Description of Penbrokeshire,* Part III, ed. Henry Owen (London, 1906), pp. 21-24.

4 *A Problem of Poverty, 1578.*

To the right worshipful Sir Edward Stradling, Knight.

This bearer (right worshipful) hath been ever an honest quiet man, and well able to live, until, now of late, by lending of his ware to sundry gentlemen, of whom some be dead, some other are become as poor as he, not able to pay; whereby he is so far indebted that he is never able to come out thereof, nor to avoid the danger of law for the payment of his creditors, by mean of a house full of children he hath from one year upwards to ten, except the relief of some good people may supply his want: in which respect her Majesty's honourable Council in the Marches have granted him a placard for pity and charity's sake to the counties of Gloucester and Glamorgan to ask the devotion of such as shall please to give him any thing; where, if it may please you at this my suit to further him with your countenance and credit amongst such of your friends as will give, you shall do undoubtedly a charitable deed, which God will reward, and assuredly bind me (if I may be further than I think myself already to be) at your commandment, either in this shire or elsewhere, in the like case for any friend of yours during life. And so, with due and most hearty commendations to you and my good lady, I wish you increase of worship in prosperous, happy, and loving life. Highnam, my poor house, near Gloucester, the 28th of July 1578.

> Your poor kinsman ever assured,
> N. ARNOLD.

From J. M. Traherne (ed.), *Stradling Correspondence* (London, 1840), pp. 198-99.

5 *Council in the Marches: Examiner's Oath.*

You shall swear that you shall faithfully and truly write the sayings and depositions of all witnesses and other persons by you to be examined for any matter in question before this Council, according to the declaration of the same witness and other persons by you to be examined.

You shall not add, alter or diminish any part of the saying of the deposit but sincerely and discreetly to set forth the same according to the verity and truth.

And finally you shall do all things as to a faithful honest and upright examiner appertaineth, not disclosing the effect of any deposition before the publication thereof . . .

From Flenley, p. 77.

6 *Corruption among Sheriffs, 1572.*

By the Queen.

Right Well beloved. Forasmuch as in past years Sheriffs for that our county have been appointed who for their worthiness and ability have well served the shire and the Commonwealth. Yet of late the Lord President and Council have understood that some of the Sheriffs, forgetting their duty and trust, have used their office to their own private gain by bargaining and compounding and receiving large sums of money for the offices of Deputy Sheriff, Shire Clerk, Bailiff of Hundreds, Jailor and other petty rooms and under offices, so leading to extortion by way of Comortha and bribery of great sums of money, goods and chattels to the impoverishment of the inhabitants of the shire, whereby divers substantial freeholders have often withdrawn from the Sessions and execution of sums recovered delayed to the damage of many of our subjects, the harm of the Commonwealth and contrary to the laws and Statutes on the subject. The Queen has therefore commanded the Lord President and Council to take measures against the sale of offices and exactions. Therefore we straightly charge you to exhibit this letter in all fairs, markets or other assemblies and if hereafter any Sheriff shall be found to have received bribes of money, goods or cattle, directly or indirectly, he shall be called before the Lord President and Council and punished by fine, imprisonment or otherwise, besides loss of his office without any chance of again filling it. The Justices of the Peace are likewise to be vigilant, notifying any breach of these commands, to the Lord President and Council. You shall make report on the proclamation of this letter, on the 31st January. Given under our Signet, Henry Sydney, John Throckmorton. C. Foxe, Raulf Barton.

From Flenley, pp. 98-99.

7 *Difficulties in preserving Law and Order, 1573.*

Whereas the Lord President and Council are given to understand that an excessive number of alehouses exists in the counties mentioned below [Wales and Monmouthshire], many being in desert and secret places, as woods, commons, waste grounds and mountains out of any highway; and the number is still increasing by the obtaining of licences from Justices of the Peace who are far away from the affected places and ignorant of the character of the applicant or the needs of the locality. And as by this felonies are increased, thieves, murderers and women of light conversation are harboured, rogues and vagabonds maintained, whoredom, filthy and detestable life much frequented, unlawful games as Tables, Dice, Cards, Bowls, Kayles, Quoits, and such like commonly exercised, Bows and Arrows left aside to the great decay of artillery and emboldening and encouragement of the foreign enemy. And as by the statute passed in the 14th year of the reign a most godly way was provided for the relief of the poor, aged and impotent, whereby they should not wander abroad but be relieved in their own parishes, the poor and needy are like to starve and rogues and vagabonds wander about unpunished by default of the Sheriffs, Justices of the Peace, Constables, Petty Constables and other under officers.

Therefore the Lord President and Council, desiring to amend this state of things, have thought to advertise those in authority that they may have regard to their credit. So letters mentioning the premises are to be dispatched to the Sheriffs and Justices of the Peace in the counties named below, ordering them to bend their whole study to the discharge of their duties. They are to assemble to discuss by what means good order may be continued, alehouses, vagabonds and unlawful games suppressed, the poor relieved, and artillery maintained . . .

From Flenley, pp. 102-3.

[8] *Precept to summon Quarter Sessions, 1552.*

28 June 1552. ·

John Wyn ap Meredydd, esquire, and his associates, Justices of the lord king assigned to keep the peace in the county of Caernarvon and to hear and determine divers felonies, trespasses and other misdemeanours perpetrated in the same county, to the sheriff of the same county, greeting. On behalf of the lord the king we order you that you omit not on account of any liberty in your bailiwick but that you enter it and cause to come before us on Monday namely the 18th day of July next to come at Caernarvon twenty four free and lawful men from each hundred, trithing, wapentake and each borough of your aforesaid bailiwick to do there what shall be enjoined upon them on behalf of the lord the king. You are also to cause all stewards, constables, subconstables, and bailiffs within hundreds and of the boroughs aforesaid that they shall then be there having with them all the names of artificers, labourers and servants within their bailiwicks taking excessive [wages] against the form of the ordinances and statutes sufficiently engrossed. Moreover you are to cause it to be proclaimed that all those who both on behalf of the lord king and on their own behalf wish to complain or prosecute against these artificers, labourers and servants any actions according to the form of the ordinances and statutes aforesaid that they shall then be there before the Justices ready to prosecute therein. And you yourself are to be there then with the bailiffs of the hundreds, liberties and boroughs aforesaid having with you all the names of the stewards, constables and subconstables, jurors and this precept. Witness being the aforesaid John Wyn at Gwydir . . .

Endorsement: Return of Hugh Peeke, esq., sheriff of the county of Caernarvon, to this writ. By virtue of this writ I cause to come before the within written Justices at the day and place within written both twelve free and lawful men from each hundred and liberty within written and twenty four free and lawful men for the body of the county of Caernarvon to do as this writ demands and requires . . .

From W. Ogwen Williams (ed.), *Calendar of the Caernarvon-shire Quarter Sessions Records,* Vol. I: 1541-58 (Caernarvon, 1956), pp..94-95 (translated from Latin).

9 *Quarter Sessions Indictment, 1557.*

7 October 1557.

Margaret ferch Ieuan ap David ap Madog of Ffestiniog in the county of Merioneth, spinster, at Clynnog feloniously stole a cheese worth 1d. and a 'test anglice a sesterne' in money by tale to the value of 6d., being the property of Lewis ap John ap William . . .

Footnote: And because she places herself and acknowledges the petty larceny aforesaid so it is adjudged by the Justices that she shall be flogged and that afterwards she is to be nailed by her ear in the market place at Caernarvon.

From Ogwen Williams, p. 159 (partly translated from Latin).

10 *A Method of Dealing with Desertion, 1573.*

To the right worshipful Sir Edward Stradling, Knight, be these delivered.

Sir, The bearer hereof, being one that dwelleth somewhat near me, hath requested me to write these few lines unto you in her behalf. That whereas she hath by the space of nine years been married to one Richard Love, by occupation a carpenter, the said Richard Love about Whitsuntide last was twelve months departed from this poor woman his wife, and took with him a lewd concubine, who hath a husband at this present dwelling at Bath. This poor woman hath been informed by some of her friends that the said Richard Love, her husband, inhabiteth in a parish somewhat near you, called Cowbridge: if, therefore, it may please you for God's sake, as also according to the laws of the realm, to show your favour to this poor woman in taking some good order with the lewd fellow her husband, no doubt you shall do a most godly deed; and myself, in this poor woman's behalf, will always be ready to be employed in these parts, or in any place elsewhere I may stand you in the like stead. Thus, as one unacquainted, do, with my hearty commendations, take my leave of you. Hasylburye, this 18th of March 1573.

Your loving friend,
JOHN CLYFTON.

From Traherne, pp. 160-61.

11 *Gentry Rivalries, 1575*
To my very loving cousin Sir Edward Stradling, Knight, give this.

Good cousin, Understanding of some disagreements and troubles lately renewed between my cousin Carne and you, and that there is on both sides great part-taking, to the grief of your friends, and rejoicing of your enemies, I have, as one that wisheth well unto either party, dealt with my cousin Carne for quietness sake, as of my self, not to follow any matter by suit of law, or complaint unto the Council, until such time as I may hear from you; hoping that as he is conformable to any reasonable end that I shall make, so you will not be against that which is so requisite and necessary amongst neighbours and friends. And for my own part rather than you should continue in this boiling hatred, I will purposely, if otherwise it can not be brought to pass, make a journey into the country to set you at unity, if my coming may do good; and that presently will I determine, upon such answer as I shall hear from you. And so, with my right hearty commendations, I bid you heartily farewell. Wilton, this second of November, 1575.

Your assured loving cousin and friend,
H. PEMBROKE.

From Traherne, pp. 65-66.

12 *The Vulnerability of Anglesey, 1558.*
By the Queen.
Whereas the Isle of Anglesey within our Principality of North Wales lies open both to France and Scotland, we have

thought good, considering the late attempt of our ancient enemies the Frenchmen and also the Scots, who are nothing ignorant of the landing places there, to foresee that there be supply of men ready at all times for the better meeting of such attempts as haply shall be offered against the said Isle. We have therefore ordered that with the inhabitants of that our country the force of Carnarvon shall be ready to aid the said isle when and where occasion arises on any attempt in any haven creek or place therein. And as we have sent letters to the Justices of Peace and Sheriffs of those counties adjoining the sea coast, so our pleasure is that you, in whom we have special trust, shall muster the inhabitants of the isle of Anglesey, willing and requiring you forthwith upon receipt of this to assemble yourselves and out of hand to muster and make ready all the able men in the said isle with furniture of armour meet for the wars, and to see that every man be ready upon all occasions to repair to the landing place when and wheresoever commanded, to repulse the enemy's sudden appearance and enterprise there. We doubt not but you will appoint such men to lead and rule as are able, as also have care to the watch of the beacons as opportunity shall serve, conferring in this matter with the commissioners of the other shires so that you and they may better win in this service, seeing in anywise that the inhabitants there rest at home for the defence of the isle.

From Flenley, pp. 49-50.

13 *Raising Men and Armour for the Army, 1579.*
To the right worshipful my especial good cousin Sir Edward Stradling, K.

I have thought it good to send this bearer, my chaplain, unto you, to know how forward you are in the setting forth of your men, and what wants you have, either of halberds or any other good furniture, and that we may make all the shift we can to supply those places. My only trust is in you for the choice of the men, both for their personage and behaviour; and that they may be reasonable furnished with necessary apparel and furniture, and some such that may carry some money with them for their relief, or otherwise they may perish for want. Also I pray you they may have reasonable allowance of powder to train them while they are on this side of the water, and on the sea in going; for God knows what may happen unto us, as it hath to our Devonshire men already, who have bought it dear, as I hear say. Their coats I would wish to be after the fashion as the coats in this country are; the which if you will, I will send you an example I think my man that was with you before had on his back. I have brought between 30 and 50 foot soldiers with me from London, [who] are reasonably furnished, whom, if it will please you to allow some good allowance to furnish them, you may have half a dozen or eight of them to spare so many of your country; and praying you to have the best consideration you may for our conduct money, seeing for that I have carried a great many of the best from London. Thus, taking my leave, I wish unto you as to my self own heart. In haste. From Pencoid, this 28th of September 1579. Your loving and assured cousin,

WILLIAM MORGAN.

From Traherne, pp. 204-5.

14 *Problems of Religious Observance, 1569.*

The Queen's Majesty has been lately informed that some of those persons in Commission of the Peace in the county of Pembroke, whose office and duty is to set forth and see maintained Her Highness' laws, ordinances and proceedings published by Her Majesty and agreed by the realm in Parliament, do nevertheless condemn and that of set purpose, to do the same in certain points concerning the state of religion established by the realm and set forth by Her Highness, as by not resorting to the Common Prayer and Divine Service, and not receiving the Holy Sacraments according to the order prescribed by law, agreeably with the ordinance of Almighty God, thereby seeking to breed and bring forth such sects and factions as be the very seeds and roots of sedition amongst Her Majesty's people and leaving (?) full of danger to the common quiet and peace of the country. For the avoiding whereof, and to the end such disordered persons, givers of evil example in this behalf, may be known from the rest that do their offices and duties faithfully and diligently, according to the commission and trust granted and reposed in them. Her Majesty hath presently charged and commanded her Council in the Marches of Wales to advertise the Sheriff and Justices of the Peace in the county of Pembroke touching the premises, and to send the tenor of the letter annexed to them, to the intent the same may be returned and subscribed by the hand of so many of them as should allow and agree to the content thereof. It is therefore ordered by Her Majesty's said Council in the Marches of Wales that a letter rehearsing the premises be directed unto the Sheriff and Justices of the Peace of the said county of Pembroke with the minute of the said letter enclosed. Requiring them forthwith upon receipt thereof to assemble themselves together at some one place or more as shall seem meet for this purpose and there communicate that Her Majesty's order and proceed in their assembly to the execution thereof. And for due satisfaction of Her Majesty those which shall willingly subscribe the same shall advertise Her Highness' said Council in the Marches of Wales, not only who they be that shall in their presence refuse to forbear to subscribe the same but shall cause also such as be absent to have knowledge thereof with charge to come to some place and to subscribe it in the presence of some of them that have subscribed. And because there may be diverse persons in that county of Pembroke of livelihood who be not presently in the Commission of the Peace, and yet have been in former times, the Queen's Majesty's pleasure is that they all at their assemblies for this purpose shall by their precept in Her Majesty's name command all such persons to appear before them all or before some convenient number of them which shall subscribe the said letter and to such persons to cause the contests of this Her Majesty's order to be declared, willing them to subscribe the same. And thereupon Her Majesty's further pleasure and commandment is that of so many of them which either be no Justices of Peace or heretofore at any time have been as refuse to subscribe, that they shall take sufficient bonds wherein every of them being a knight shall be bound to the

Queen's Majesty's use in the sum of £200 and being an esquire in the sum of 200 marks to be and remain of good havering [behaviour] and also to appear before the Lords of Her Majesty's most honourable Privy Council attending Her person whensoever they shall be warned so to do. And of their doings in performing the premises to advertise the said Council in the Marches within 30 days after the receipt of the same letters to the end the same Council may advertise Her Majesty thereof, and thereof not to fail as they tender Her Highness' pleasure.

Like several letters to the Sheriffs and Justices of the Peace of the several counties of Carmarthen, Cardigan, Glamorgan, Brecknock, Radnor, Montgomery, Denbigh, Flint, Merioneth, Carnarvon, Anglesey. And another letter of like tenor to the Mayor, Sheriff and Justices of the Peace of the town and county of Haverfordwest.

From Flenley, pp. 58-59.

Bibliographical Note

A. *Introductory.*

Important documentary material on Elizabethan government is available in G. R. Elton, *The Tudor Constitution* (1960), and there are relevant documents in J. Hurstfield and A. G. R. Smith, *Elizabethan People. State and Society* (1972). An ideal general introduction is A. G. R. Smith, *The Government of Elizabethan England* (1967), while there are useful chapters in A. L. Rowse, *The England of Elizabeth* (1950). More specialist aspects are dealt with in W. T. Mac-Caffrey, 'Place and Patronage in Elizabethan Politics', in *Elizabethan Government and Society,* eds. S. T. Bindoff, J. Hurstfield and C. H. Williams (1961), and *The Shaping of the Elizabethan Regime* (1969); J. Hurstfield, *Elizabeth I and the Unity of England* (1960); J. E. Neale, *The Elizabethan House of Commons* (1949), and *Elizabeth and her Parliaments* (2 vols., 1953 and 1957); and C. G. Cruickshank, *Elizabeth's Army* (2nd. ed., 1966). On specific offices, reference must be made to G. Scott Thompson, *Lords Lieutenant in the Sixteenth Century* (1923), and William Lambarde's *Eirenarcha* (1581) on the J.P.

B. *Wales*

There is a wide range of documentary material available, including George Owen, 'Dialogue of the Government of Wales' in *The Description of Penbrokeshire,* ed. Henry Owen (Cymmrodorion Record Series, no. 1, 4 vols., 1902-36); Ralph Flenley (ed.), *A Calendar of the Register of the Queen's Majesty's Council in the dominion and principality of Wales and the Marches of the same [1535], 1569-1591*

(1916); Rice Merrick, *A Booke of Glamorganshires Antiquities, 1578,* ed. J. A. Corbett (1887); W. O. Williams (ed.), *Calendar of the Caernarvonshire Quarter Sessions Records* vol. I [1541-1558] (1956); Sir John Wynn *The History of the Gwydir family,* ed. J. Ballinger (1927); J. M. Traherne (ed.), *Stradling Correspondence* (1840); J. Ballinger (ed.), *Calendar of Wynn (of Gwydir) Papers, 1515-1690* (1926); T. Jones Pierce (ed.), *Clenennau Letters and Papers in the Brogyntyn Collection* (1947). The full text of the acts of Union is available in I. Bowen (ed.), *Statutes of Wales* (1908).

Hugh Thomas, *A History of Wales, 1485-1660* (1972), is the most recent textbook on the period and can be complemented by David Williams, *A History of Modern Wales* (1950), and A. J. Roderick (ed.), *Wales through the Ages,* vol. II (1960). Important material on the emergence and status of the gentry is available in W. O. Williams, 'The Social Order in Tudor Wales', in *Transactions of the Honourable Society of Cymmrodorion [T.H.S.C.],* 1967, and A. H. Dodd, 'The Social Order', in his *Studies in Stuart Wales* (1971). The most important single contribution to the study of Welsh government and politics in the period is Penry Williams, *The Council in the Marches of Wales under Elizabeth I* (1958). Indispensable also are his articles on 'The Welsh Borderland under Queen Elizabeth', *Welsh History Review,* I (1960), and 'The Political and Administrative History of Glamorgan, 1536-1642', in Glanmor Williams (ed.), *Glamorgan County History,* IV (1974). W. O. Williams, *Tudor Gwynedd* (1958), provides further information. Parts of G. D. Owen, *Elizabethan Wales. The Social Scene* (1962), are relevant, while A. H. Dodd has an article on 'Wales's Parliamentary Apprenticeship (1536-1625)', *T.H.S.C.,* 1942. T. H. Lewis's articles on 'The Justice of the Peace in Wales', and 'The Administration of Justice in the Welsh County in its Relation to other organs of Justice, Higher and Lower', in *T.H.S.C.,* 1943-44 and 1945, might also be consulted.

The most comprehensive account of the Welsh gentry is H. A. Lloyd, *The Gentry of South-West Wales, 1540-1640* (1968). Brian Howells has an informative essay on 'The Eliza-

bethan Squirearchy in Pembrokeshire', in *The Pembrokeshire Historian,* I (1959). Short biographies of the more important gentlemen are available in the *Dictionary of Welsh
Biography* (1959). There is a particularly useful biography of
George Owen of Henllys (1973) by B. G. Charles. Religious
affiliations of the gentry have been discussed by Glanmor
Williams in *Welsh Reformation Essays* (1967), and E. G.
Jones, *Cymru a'r Hen Ffydd* (1951); while W. O. Williams
has investigated 'The Survival of the Welsh language after
the Union of England and Wales: the First Phase, 1536-
1642', in *Welsh History Review,* II (1964). P. R. Roberts
'The Union with England and the Identity of "Anglican"
Wales', *Transactions of the Royal Historical Society, 1972,*
sets a number of themes of this book in perspective.

Index

111

estate-building, 22, 23, 31, 34, 38, 40.
Exchequer, Court of, 47, 48, 51, 52,
   54, 66, 93.

faction, 24, 25, 34, 94.
feuds, 17, 26, 46, 47.
Fleming, John, 13.
Flintshire, 70, 86.
Franklin, Jenkin, 70.
Froude, Charles, 49, 50. .

Gamage, family of Coity, 25.
   Robert, of Coity, 80.
genealogy, 20, 21, 26, 30, 33, 36, 37.
gentry, definition of, 30, 32, 33.
   rivalries of, 18, 44, 79, 81, 94.
   resources of, 31-33.
Glamorgan, 13-15, 20, 21, 24-26, 32,
   37, 38, 40, 41, 43, 54, 64, 70, 73, 74-
   76, 79-81, 83, 84, 86, 93.
Gloucestershire, 53.
Glyndŵr, Owain, 28, 31.
grammar schools, 91.
Great Sessions, Court of, 48, 51, 57
   59, 63, 72, 75, 90, 94.
Griffith, Capt. Hugh, 82, 83.
Griffith, John, 83.
Gruffydd ap Nicholas, 29.
Gwyneth, Rees, 35.
Gwynne, Richard, 56.

Haverfordwest, 33, 42.
Hawkins, Nicholas, 49, 50, 66, 67.
Henry IV, 21, 23, 31.
Henry VII, 22, 23, 31, 40.
Henry VIII, 40.
Herbert family, 25, 46, 65, 69.
   Sir George, of Swansea, 34, 46, 80.
   Nicholas, of Cardiff, 49, 50, 68, 70,
   74.
   Sir William, of Swansea, 49, 50, 54,
   62, 67, 68, 74, 81.
   William, of Cogan Pill, 80.
Herefordshire, 51, 53.
Historie of Cambria, 20.
History of the Gwydir Family, 39.
Holyhead, 47, 52, 61.
House of Commons, 42, 43, 85.
Howard, Lord, of Effingham, 26, 38.
Hughes, John, of Cardiff, 65.
hundred courts, 21, 63.
hundreds, 71.

inflation, 31, 93.
inns of court, 33, 37, 39, 91.
invasion, 44, 56, 61.
Ireland, 16, 36, 40, 61, 62, 78, 79.
Italy, 82.

Jenkin, David ap, of Llangatwg, 81.
Jones, Sir Thomas, 62.
juries, 49, 51, 67-69, 72.
justices of the peace, 14, 15, 17, 32, 33,
   35, 37, 40, 41, 44, 47, 48, 50, 55-58,
   62, 64, 65, 69-73, 83, 84, 87, 93.
justiciar, 29.

Kemeys, Edward, of Cefn Mabli, 64-
   70, 87.
Kenfig, 81.
King's Bench, Court of, 48.

Lancashire, 86.
law and order, 23, 64, 71-75, 93, 94.
lay impropriation, 87, 88.
Leicester, Robert Dudley, earl of, 24-
   26, 29, 55.
Leland, John, 20.
Lewis, family of Y Fan, 65.
   Dr David, 75, 76.
   Edward, of Y Fan, 80, 86.
   Thomas, of Y Fan, 70, 86.
litigation, 39, 51, 54.
Llandaff, bishop of, 73.
   diocese of, 86.
Llandovery, 43.
Lloyd, Hugh, 51, 52, 54.
   Sir John, of Bodidras, 15, 16.
Lluyd, Humphrey, 21.
Llyn peninsula, 84, 86, 93.
London, 14, 17, 78, 82, 90.
   Tower of, 14, 46.
lord lieutenant, 23, 60, 61.
Ludlow, 57, 78, 90.

manorial courts, 21.
Mansel, family of Margam, 25, 40, 41,
   47.
   Ann, 46.
   Anthony, 70, 86.
   Sir Edward, 41, 46, 65, 70.
   Sir Rice, 25, 40, 41.
   Sir Thomas, 47, 54, 75.
marcher lords, 29.
Margam estates, 40.